Developing Games on the Raspberry Pi

App Programming with Lua and LÖVE

Seth Kenlon

Apress®

Developing Games on the Raspberry Pi: App Programming with Lua and LÖVE

Seth Kenlon
Wellington, New Zealand

ISBN-13 (pbk): 978-1-4842-4169-1   ISBN-13 (electronic): 978-1-4842-4170-7
https://doi.org/10.1007/978-1-4842-4170-7

Library of Congress Control Number: 2018966138

Managing Director, Apress Media LLC: Welmoed Spahr
Acquisitions Editor: Aaron Black
Development Editor: James Markham
Coordinating Editor: Jessica Vakili

Cover image designed by Freepik (www.freepik.com)

Distributed to the book trade worldwide by Springer Science+Business Media New York, 233 Spring Street, 6th Floor, New York, NY 10013. Phone 1-800-SPRINGER, fax (201) 348-4505, e-mail orders-ny@springer-sbm.com, or visit www.springeronline.com. Apress Media, LLC is a California LLC and the sole member (owner) is Springer Science + Business Media Finance Inc (SSBM Finance Inc). SSBM Finance Inc is a **Delaware** corporation.

For information on translations, please e-mail rights@apress.com, or visit http://www.apress.com/rights-permissions.

Apress titles may be purchased in bulk for academic, corporate, or promotional use. eBook versions and licenses are also available for most titles. For more information, reference our Print and eBook Bulk Sales web page at http://www.apress.com/bulk-sales.

Any source code or other supplementary material referenced by the author in this book is available to readers on GitHub via the book's product page, located at www.apress.com/978-1-4842-4169-1. For more detailed information, please visit http://www.apress.com/source-code.

Printed on acid-free paper

This book is dedicated to all programmers who work tirelessly on free (as in "liberty") and open software, not the least of whom are the Lua devs.

Table of Contents

TABLE OF CONTENTS

About the Author

Seth Kenlon is a teacher, artist, D&D dungeon master, free software and free culture advocate, and UNIX geek. He has worked in the visual effects (VFX) (*The Hobbit, Deadpool, Valerian*) and computing industries (IBM, Red Hat), often at the same time. He is one of the maintainers of a Slackware-based multimedia production project.

About the Technical Reviewer

Sai Yamanoor is an IoT (Internet of Things) applications engineer working for an industrial gases company in Buffalo, NY. His interests, deeply rooted in DIY and open-source hardware, include developing gadgets that aid behavior modification. He has published two books with his brother and in his spare time, he likes to contribute to open source projects. You can find his project portfolio at `http://saiyamanoor.com`.

CHAPTER 1

Getting Started with the Raspberry Pi

Welcome to the exciting world of the Raspberry Pi and the Lua programming language. Whether you're already a programmer looking to learn about Lua, or the proud but confused new owner of a Raspberry Pi looking for a fun project, or a budding freelancer looking to get into mobile app development, or just a curious computer user looking to learn more, this book is your gateway into an exciting new world of fun with software.

To get through this book, you'll use two main tools: Lua and the Raspberry Pi.

Note   This book requires no previous experience with computers or programming. Everything you need to know, you can learn from this book and diligent practice.

Lua is a small, fast, modern programming language that can be used for everything from system maintenance to graphics and standalone games. It's a leading scripting language in the video game and visual effects industry, and it is used for front-end development in several popular game engines. Learning Lua is not only a great way to learn programming, it's a pathway into the software development industry.

© Seth Kenlon 2019
S. Kenlon, *Developing Games on the Raspberry Pi*,
https://doi.org/10.1007/978-1-4842-4170-7_1

The Raspberry Pi is, of course, a groundbreaking computer roughly the size of a mobile phone. It costs just $35 USD. Against all odds, the non-profit Raspberry Pi Foundation competes with dominating mega-corporations by selling an educational product loaded with open source software to students, teachers, and hobbyists like you. It's a great, affordable way to learn programming, open source, and how computers really work.

You may have acquired a Raspberry Pi for any variety of reasons, but here are the reasons that it was a good choice, and why it's the platform that this book uses:

- The Pi uses the ARM architecture, as opposed to the x86 architecture made popular by AMD and Intel. Most mobile phones use ARM chips, and mobile technology is the fastest-growing market for games. You don't have to develop games on ARM to publish games for mobile, but if you believe that knowing technology starts with using that technology, then $35 for a mobile game dev kit is a smart investment.

- The Raspberry Pi runs Linux, a free version of UNIX. You might not know UNIX yet, but if you're heading into the tech industry, the more you know about it, the better. UNIX knowledge is invaluable because most of the Internet is run on it, and it's the basis for Android phones, Steam machines, the PlayStation 4, and most of the film and TV visual FX industry. Besides that, it's a lot of fun.

- When computers first came out, it was expected that they would be tools that people could use to bring their ideas to life. It didn't matter whether your idea was great or small, you could make a computer do what you wanted it to do.

- Computers today are largely struggling to meet that goal. While programming on a Mac or a Windows PC is common, access to the full OS is restricted, and it can be expensive to keep up with the latest releases. There shouldn't be a barrier into computing. Use this book, a Raspberry Pi, and your passion for creativity and discovery to prove that programming is still for everyone.

- You can learn Windows or you can learn macOS, and either way, you learn either Windows or macOS. If you learn Linux, however, you learn *computing*. There will always be differences in how different platforms work, but an open source system like Linux lets you gain familiarity with the low-level computational basics shared by all computers, whether desktop, laptop, or mobile.

Preparing Your Pi

Believe it or not, one of the strengths of the Raspberry Pi is that it is low power. If you develop on a low-powered computer, then you broaden your audience because not everyone has the latest and greatest gaming rig or mobile device. Indeed, developing on a Pi is perfect for targeting the mobile market, because the Pi shares a lot with the internal hardware of mobile phones.

In the same spirit of inclusiveness, you don't actually have to have a Raspberry Pi to follow along with this book. You can buy any System-on-a-Chip (SoC) device; common ones include the BeagleBone, Banana Pi, Odroid, and the Pine64.

This book is general enough to cover whatever SoC device you use and any Linux or UNIX operating system. Technically, you can even use a spare computer instead, although you'll need to install Linux on it first or boot from a Linux USB drive. The important thing is to get through this section and end up with some computing device loaded with a UNIX or Linux operating system.

The advantage of a genuine Raspberry Pi is that it is thoroughly documented. There are lots of tutorials on raspberrypi.org to help you through anything you don't understand, and there's little to no variation in what you see on a Pi compared to what you see in this book.

Depending on where you buy your Raspberry Pi, you might find that the OS (called either Raspbian or NOOBS) is included in the box. That's fine for normal use, but when programming, it's best to have access to the latest development libraries. Raspbian isn't known for providing the most recent software tools, so this book uses a Linux OS called Fedberry, derived from the popular Fedora distribution of Linux. You can either purchase a spare microSD card to use with this book, or use the microSD card that came with your Pi, as long as you accept that the contents of your card will be replaced with a different OS.

If you purchased a Raspberry Pi that didn't include the OS on an SD card, or if you purchased a different SoC device that doesn't come already set up, then you have a computer that doesn't know what to do when you turn it on. It needs an operating system, and it's a great learning experience for you to install one.

Installing Linux onto Your Pi with Etcher

To install an operating system on your Pi or SoC device, you need a microSD card and an OS image file. OS images are available from fedberry.org/#download. Use the Fedberry "minimal" image file.

Caution   This process *erases* the card, so don't use one containing photos, videos, or other data that you care about.

There are many ways to get a disk image onto a microSD card. The following is the easy method, and it's the same whether you run Linux, macOS, or Windows on your personal computer.

1. If you have not already done so, download the Fedberry LXQT image from `https://github.com/fedberry/fedberry/releases`. This image provides a basic OS with a few extra applications. You will manually install a full development environment later.

2. On your personal computer, download and install the Etcher application from `www.balena.io/etcher/`. For both Etcher and Fedberry, you need a tool to unzip archives. If you run Linux on your personal computer, then you already have one; otherwise, download and install 7zip from `www.7-zip.org` for Windows or Keka from `www.keka.io` for macOS.

3. Put the microSD card into your computer. If your computer doesn't have an SD card slot, you must purchase a microSD card reader.

4. Once the OS image has downloaded and Etcher has been installed, launch the Etcher application.

5. In the Etcher window, select the Fedberry image file from where it is saved on your hard drive, probably in your `Downloads` directory (see Figure 1-1).

5

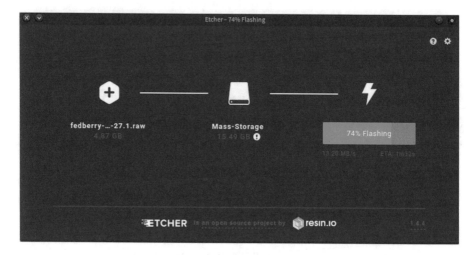

Figure 1-1. *Etcher in action*

6.   Select the SD card as the destination.

7.   And finally, click the Flash button.

You can now skip to the "Writing Your First Lua Script" section.

Preparing Your Off-Brand SoC

If you only have a SoC board that is not made by the Raspberry Pi Foundation, then the OS images for the Raspberry Pi probably won't work on your device. But you can still use this book!

Your first step is to visit the website of your device's manufacturer. They probably offer an OS for the device they produce, and since they are targeting their own device, the OS image is likely a prebuilt image to copy to your SD card using the Etcher application. This process is described in *Installing Linux onto your Pi with Etcher.*

If you cannot find an official image for your device, the next step is to do an Internet search for the name of your device plus a query such as "Linux image". It helps to know which chip your device is based upon, too, since sometimes generic OS images target the chip rather than every possible brand name applied to a system built around that chip. Whether you have an Allwinner, armv6, armv7, Tegra, or something else entirely, there's a good chance that somewhere on the Internet, there are a few hardworking hackers supporting your device.

Finally, if all else fails, you can turn to the two most reliable OS providers in the modern world: Debian Linux and NetBSD. These groups justifiably pride themselves on providing an operating system that runs on nearly every device you can think to put an OS onto (and a few that you wouldn't).

Debian Linux is available from debian.org. Depending on your device, you may have to do a little research on `wiki.debian.org/InstallingDebianOn` to understand how an install is done, but the good news is that it's almost certainly possible.

NetBSD is available from `wiki.netbsd.org/ports/evbarm`. The install process for NetBSD is remarkably easy, but the setup afterward is considerably more complex, especially if you're not familiar with UNIX yet.

If this is the route you are taking, you should take a little extra time to set up your system and to get familiar with it before continuing this book. The instructions in this book are mostly universal, but instructions on installing software or configuring sound outputs and other details may differ depending on your device and operating system.

Using This Book Without a SoC Device

If you don't have and cannot get a Raspberry Pi or other SoC, then you can use a traditional computer to work through this book, even a very old one. You'll get all the same benefits as those using a Pi: you'll learn programming, you'll learn Linux, and you'll learn all about the software development process, but you will have to work a little harder to get set up.

To set up a computer to use with this book, install Fedora Linux from `spins.fedoraproject.org/en/lxqt/` so that your environment mirrors the one in this book.

Caution   This *erases* all the content on your computer, so use a spare computer that doesn't contain data you care about.

It's out of the scope of this book, but there are many ways to run Linux on a computer, and technically, any of them are probably acceptable for this book. For instance, you can run Linux off of a USB drive or DVD using porteus.org, or you can run Linux in a virtual machine using virtualbox.org. Whatever you choose, you have to translate what is in this book for what you are using. In other words, it's easier to just get a Pi and follow along, but it's not strictly required.

If this is the route you are taking, you should take a little extra time to set up your system and to get familiar with it before continuing this book. The instructions in this book are mostly universal, but instructions on installing software or configuring sound outputs and other details may differ, depending on your device and operating system.

First Boot

Assuming that you have your Pi plugged into a monitor, keyboard, mouse, and Ethernet, you can finally boot into your fresh, new Linux operating system. The first time you boot, you are asked to configure your system.

1. Configure your network to connect wirelessly to the Internet. If you are connected to the Internet over an Ethernet cable, then you can skip this category.

2. Set your time zone. To have your Pi get the correct time and day from the Internet, enable NTP in the upper-right corner of the time zone screen.

3. Set the administrative password.

4. Create a user and set a user password. Set the
    user as an administrator (see Figure 1-2). Take
    note of your username and password. You will
    need them often!

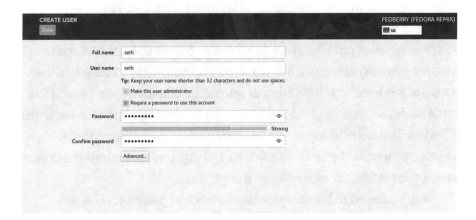

Figure 1-2. *Setting up FedBerry with the Anaconda installer*

5. Click the **Finish Configuration** button in the bottom
    right of the main screen to continue booting.

Note   From this point on, the term *Pi* is meant to encompass
whatever device you are using to follow along with this book.

When Fedberry has booted, you are left at the login screen. You'll log in
to the desktop soon, but you got this book so that you could learn to code,
so it's worth looking behind the scenes. Press Ctrl+Alt+F3 to switch to a
text login screen instead.

Writing Your First Lua Script

The modern computing public likes to think that computers have evolved into interactive virtual worlds, but programmers know the truth: computers— whether it's a server, a desktop, or a mobile phone—are merely highly efficient calculators that get instructions in the form of *plain text*. When you switch a Linux computer to a text console, you're seeing the not-so-secret side of the operating system that responds to text commands. That's great if you're an experienced UNIX user, but it can be crippling if you don't know what commands exist, much less which commands to use. Throughout the course of this book, you'll get familiar with useful commands for Linux. Most commands you learn apply to any UNIX system, although some are particular to Fedora. Instead of listing common commands and expecting you to memorize them, however, this book uses and explains commands throughout so that you get familiar with them by using them.

First, you need to log in with a username and password. Use the username and user password that you created during setup. When you type in your password, it *appears* that nothing is happening; that's to be expected, just keep typing.

Once you're logged in, you are given a shell prompt that ends with a dollar sign ($). This means that your computer is ready for a command.

To program in Lua, you need to have Lua installed. In Linux, most of the "obvious" software that users need is stored in repositories of applications on remote servers. You can think of it as an app store (although it predates app stores by at least a decade).

Fedberry includes Lua by default, but this is a good exercise nevertheless, as it demonstrates how to confirm that an application you need is indeed installed.

The Fedora dnf command searches and installs software from Fedberry repositories. You will use this command a lot throughout this book, so you will become familiar with it, but for now just type this:

```
$ sudo dnf install lua
```

Enter your password when prompted. Remember, when you type your password, the cursor won't move.

Note   If you installed a different OS onto your Pi, then the command is probably different. For example, on NetBSD the command is pkg_ add lua53. Refer to the OS image's documentation for help.

For your first foray into Lua, you're going to program a simple dice-rolling game that pits the user against the computer to see who can roll the highest number on a 20-sided virtual die.

So far, you've been controlling your computer with a language called Bash. To switch to Lua, launch a Lua interpreter by typing

```
$ lua
```

It may not look that different, but you probably notice that your shell prompt has changed from a $ to a > symbol. Not all programming languages have an interactive prompt like this, but it's a good way to get to know a language before embarking on a big project with it.

Programming languages have lots of built-in functions that you can use. These functions are called *methods* or, unsurprisingly, *functions*. They are organized into libraries.

For instance, the print() function in Lua's basic library prints text to the screen. Try this:

```
> print("hello world")
hello world
```

You can also have Lua print numbers.

```
> print(23)
23
> print(21+(378/18))
42.0
```

Or both.

```
> print("The answer is "..21+(378/18))
The answer is 42.0
```

Rolling Virtual Dice

For your first program, you need random numbers so that you can mimic a die roll competition. Computers are producing numbers all the time, but how do you access those numbers? Can you think of something within a computer's normal routine that would produce numbers? If you can't think of anything, try looking up from your screen at the room around you. Is there anything in your physical space that could provide a more or less random number at a glance?

After some thought, you might realize that computers usually keep track of time, just like a clock in the real world does. It's not perfect, but it's a reliable source of numbers.

Lua has many libraries filled with specialized functions. The os library contains the time function, which returns the current time, in seconds, since 1 January 1970 (the UNIX Epoch). That's a lot of numbers, especially in the context of a dice game where you only need up to 20. Setting that aside for now, try using the os.time() function yourself.

```
> os.time()
1524967695
```

When you use a function, you are "calling" it. The empty parentheses at the end of the os.time() function call allows you to send information to the function when calling it. The os.time() function doesn't require any information from you to do its job, so the parentheses are left empty. Functions like print(), and other advanced functions that you will use later (some of which you yourself will write), require more information.

There are a few problems with using os.time() as a stand-in for a die roll. The os.time() function returns a very large number, and it's not very random.

There are a few ways to take a large number and reduce it to something within a given range. One easy way uses grade school math: take any number and divide it by your maximum desired value, and use the remainder (the "modulo" in computer terminology) as your result. For instance, if you have the number 103 and divide it by 20, you get 5 with a modulo of 3. In computer science, the % sign is used to do division and return only the modulo. Try it in Lua.

```
> 103%20
3
> os.time()%20
6
> os.time()%20
12
```

The modulo of os.time() has some degree of variance, depending on the time at which you call it. This introduces a perception of randomness. You can test this by trying to predict what your "roll" will be just before calling os.time(). It's pretty difficult to predict.

Note Press the up arrow on your keyboard to recall the previous Lua function call without all the typing.

After trying to predict your roll 20 or 30 times, do you see any problems or patterns in the os.time() solution?

You might notice that making the same call to os.time() in rapid succession betrays its very predictable pattern of incrementing steadily once per second.

CHAPTER 1   GETTING STARTED WITH THE RASPBERRY PI

Using Variables and User Input

Computers are programmed. They don't exactly produce random events, because they only do exactly as they have been programmed. Yet few computers are dormant; usually, they have been programmed to interact and respond to human input. There's nothing quite as unpredictable as the human mind, so why not use it to introduce some randomness to the dice roll?

It's too obvious to just ask the human player for a random number, especially if they know the goal of the game. If you know the goal of a game is to roll 20 on a virtual 20-sided die, then any good gamer is going to "randomly" choose 20 the majority of the time. So instead, you can ask your human player for some input and then use that input as a seed of randomness.

Ignoring that this is happening on a computer in a programming language you don't know yet, try to think of some ways you could trick a player into providing you with a random value.

Here are some ideas:

- Ask the user to provide a three-digit number and add it to os.time() as an offset.

- Ask the user for two numbers. Use the difference between the two numbers as an offset.

- Ask the user for the name of an animal or a color. Count the number of letters in the answer and use that number as an offset.

- Ask for two numbers, divide their sum by 20, and use the modulo as the offset.

14

You can probably imagine even more ways, but to implement any of them, you need to know how to get input from your user. As you might guess, getting input from a user is a common task in programming, so Lua has a function for that as a part of its input/output library, called io. The problem is that Lua doesn't inherently know what to do with input. Watch what happens if you use the read function, and then type hello world as input.

```
> io.read()
hello world
hello world
```

Lua just repeats what you give it. That's not very useful, and that's exactly why variables were invented. A variable is like an empty box, and you can put anything into the box that you need to store for later. You can put a word (or *string* in programming lingo), a number, or even an image or sound effect. Variables are surprisingly easy to set and easy to use once you need them.

```
> seed=io.read()
103
> seed%20
3.0
```

A new variable, in this example called seed, is created because you use the = after a word that Lua otherwise does not recognize. Whatever io. read gets from the user is placed into the variable you created. From then on, you can call the variable just as you call functions, and use whatever is inside.

Using variables, you can create interactive applications. Write a dice-rolling application based on your new understanding of variables. Of course, since you're running Lua as an interactive session, your program gets written and runs all at the same time, but that's enough for a proof of concept.

Here is a version of a simple dice rolling game:

```
> computer=os.time()
> seed=io.read()
104
> player=os.time()+seed
> print("The computer rolled "..computer%20)
The computer rolled 6
> print("You rolled "..player%20)
You rolled 18.0
```

You have written your first fully functional program! It's not a fancy game, and the only way to play it is to type it manually into a Lua prompt, but the logic and the results are sound. In the next chapter, you will create a Lua script file so that a more advanced version of this simple dice game can be run like a normal application. In the meantime, practice creating and using variables, and try to come up with alternative random number engines.

When you're ready to leave the Lua prompt, call the Lua exit function.

```
> os.exit()
```

When you see a $ prompt again, you're back at your Bash shell.

To power off your Pi for the day, use the poweroff command.

```
$ sudo poweroff
```

Homework

I may as well admit to you that Lua actually already has a random number function as part of its math library. Like your own versions of random number generation, it too requires a seed, but it uses a lot of math tricks and entropy to generate a number within whatever range you specify. Here's how it works:

```
> math.randomseed(os.time())
> math.random(1,20)
6
> math.random(1,20)
11
> math.random(1,20)
1
> math.random(1,20)
17
```

How did I find out that Lua had a random number function? How can you find out what other features Lua has that I haven't told you about? The answer to both questions is documentation.

Any good programming language is fully documented so that programmers know what the language can do. You're a programmer now, so you should browse through Lua's reference manual, available at lua.org/manual/5.3/#index. Much of it won't make sense to you yet, and there are several conventions of code documentation that can be confusing, but knowing where to find the functions available to you is a hugely important part of learning to code.

Here are some challenges for you. Use the Lua documentation to find the answers.

- One of the ideas for tricking the user into providing a random number was to ask the user for the name of an animal and to count the letters of whatever the user typed. How would you find the length of a string in Lua?

- Find the cosine of a number provided by the user. You can do this even if you have no idea what a cosine is.

- Write a program that takes an input string from the user and then prints that string in capital (uppercase) letters. There's a way to do this both with and without a variable.

Don't worry about getting these exercises right or wrong. The important thing is to try, because trying means that you are practicing, and practice is the only way to really learn how to code. When you feel ready, or you just get bored of trying these exercises, continue to the next chapter.

CHAPTER 2

Scripting with LÖVE

In the previous chapter, you got your Pi or SoC device to boot, and then explored Lua from an interactive text console. That's more than some first-year computer science students learn about how computers work, so consider yourself a success. There's a lot more to learn, but first, it's time to set up a development environment.

Establishing a Development Environment

Having a development environment means having all the tools you need to develop software, and having a place where you can do that development without affecting the rest of your system or letting the rest of your system affect your work.

Navigating the Desktop

Log in to your Pi using the same username and password as before. If you've never used a Linux desktop before, you'll find that it's similar to any other computer (see Figure 2-1).

© Seth Kenlon 2019
S. Kenlon, *Developing Games on the Raspberry Pi*,
https://doi.org/10.1007/978-1-4842-4170-7_2

Figure 2-1. *The LXQT desktop*

An application menu is located in the bottom left corner, but the three most common applications are pinned to the panel along the bottom. The first icon is for a terminal, which is software that emulates the text console you used in the first chapter. The second icon is a file manager. With it, you can create new folders, move and copy files, move old files to the trash, browse and launch applications, and so on. The third icon is a web browser (see Figure 2-2).

Figure 2-2. *Your basic applications*

There are also some unique features developed by Linux that are slowly making their way to other platforms. For instance, in the lower-left corner, there are two boxes labeled 1 and 2. These represent virtual desktops. You can open a few applications while on desktop 1, and then switch to desktop 2 to open another application to avoid clutter. It can be useful to leave a Bash shell open on one desktop so you can run commands or test out Lua functions while your code editor is open on another desktop.

Installing Development Applications

You won't be programming complex games in the Lua prompt, as you did for your simple dice game, so you need all the usual programming tools that software developers use on a daily basis. There are lots of tools that a programmer might use, depending on what a project demands, but there are some things that are expected no matter what. These include the following.

- *Text editor.* A person who codes needs an application to write code in. Most programmers use a special kind of text editor called an *integrated development environment* (IDE), which not only edits text but also knows enough about the language being used to add convenience features, such as word completion, syntax highlighting, and file management. Popular IDEs include Eclipse, Qt Creator, and NetBeans. This book uses Geany, a lightweight IDE.

- *Terminal.* It's helpful to have direct access to the platform you're programming. A terminal gives you a shell prompt as an application inside your desktop. No more switching back to a text console with Ctrl+Alt+F3! There are many terminal emulators for Linux; this book uses QTerminal.

- *Git.* Programming is all about iteration. You try something, test it, improve it, and then try it again. With so many iterations, it's helpful to have a historical record of each attempt you make at solving a problem. Git is the basis for popular sites like GitLab and GitHub, so it's a good version control system to learn. There are many interfaces to Git. This book uses a plain old terminal as well as git-cola.

- *Web browser.* If you are going to refer to the Lua reference manual, you need a way to access the Internet. Fedberry provides the Chromium browser, the open source basis for Google's Chrome.

- *Software catalog.* To make it easy to find software, Fedberry provides the dnfdragora repository browser.

That's not all you'll need to complete this book, but it's a good start for now.

There's a lot of great software out there for Linux, so you could search for packages by description and then try each one out until you find the one you like best. You are encouraged to do that sometime when you have a free month or two, but for the sake of efficiency, install these fine applications:

```
$ sudo dnf install geany vte291 git-cola
```

If you prefer to work in graphical applications, click the application menu in the bottom left of the screen and select Administration ➤ dnfdragora.

In the dnfdragora window, set the search scope to **All**, **All**, and **in names**. The first time dnfdragora launches, it syncs with the application servers, so give it some time to pull an updated application list from the Internet. When it's finished, the main panel is populated with a list of applications.

Once the applications are listed, search for each of these installer packages: geany, vte291, and git-cola. Mark each one for installation (see Figure 2-3) and then click the Apply button in the lower-left corner of the dnfdragora window.

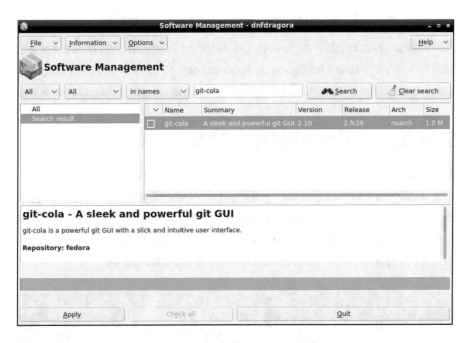

Figure 2-3. *The dnfdragora application installer*

Exploring Your Desktop

Before you start the next section, take some time to explore your desktop. Here are some things you might try:

- Launch the Chromium web browser, download a desktop wallpaper from the Internet, and set it as your desktop background.

- Try to locate hidden files in your home directory. Don't do anything with them, just learn how to view and hide them again.

- Customize some of the settings of your desktop, like the position of the panel, or the fonts used in window titles, and so on.

- Learn to use virtual desktops fluidly and also how to switch between active applications.

Getting comfortable with your workstation is important, and there's no limit to the ways that Linux can be customized. Explore your new world, and when you're feeling at home and ready to code, start the next section.

Creating a Graphical Game

The dice game you experimented with in the previous chapter demonstrated some of the very basic principles of code, but now it's time to program a game with graphics, and that someone else can play without having to type the code first. To keep things simple, the next exercise is a revised, graphical version (see Figure 2-4) of the dice game.

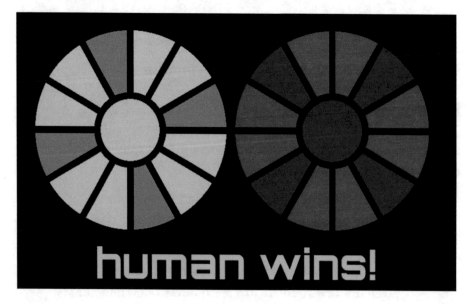

Figure 2-4. *Your very first graphical game in Lua*

You may as well start off with proper organization, so create a folder (or *directory* in UNIX terminology) for your first Lua project.

You can do this two different ways. Maybe the most obvious way is just as you would on any computer you're used to: click the file manager icon in the lower-left corner of the desktop panel to open a window to your home directory, and then right-click in the empty space of the window and choose Create New ➤ Folder. Name your new directory `dice`.

The other way is slightly faster. Launch a terminal from the application menu on the left end of the shelf at the bottom of the screen. In the terminal window, type

```
$ mkdir ~/dice
```

Remember that the $ is your shell prompt, so don't type that. The tilde (~) character is shorthand meaning *your home directory*, and the slash (/) serves as a path delimiter between one directory (your home in this case) and another (in this case, `dice`).

Whatever way you choose, the end result is a new directory in your home, called `dice`. This is where the data files for this, your first game, must be stored.

You are going to write your code in your IDE called Geany. Launch Geany now from the application menu (in the Programming category). Alternatively, you can launch it from a terminal, if you have one open, as follows:

```
$ geany&
```

Note   The & character tells your shell to launch an application and then returns you to your shell prompt. Sometimes when debugging, it's useful to leave off the & so that you maintain a link with the running application and get to see any messages that it sends.

The Geany IDE is highly configurable, with many themes and plugins. You can spend time customizing it, but at the very least click the Tools menu and select Plugin Manager. In the Plugin Manager window, activate the File Browser extension to add a display of your files in the left panel.

Additionally, go to the Edit menu and select Plugin Preferences. In the Plugin Preferences window, enable the file browser to follow the path of the current file (see Figure 2-5).

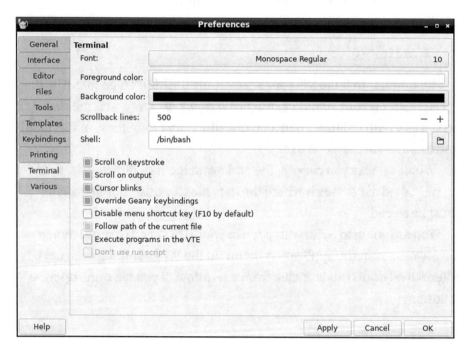

Figure 2-5. *Geany's file browser preferences*

Finally, select Preferences from the Edit menu and enable the same feature for Geany's built-in terminal (see Figure 2-6).

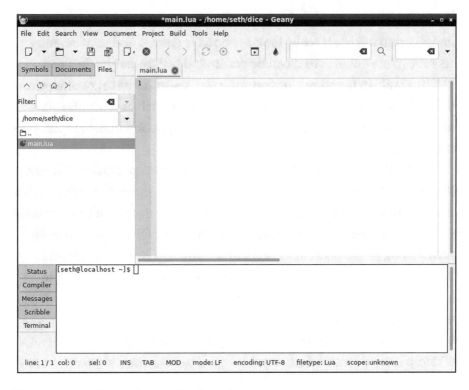

Figure 2-6. *Geany's terminal settings*

With these features activated, both the file browser and the terminal synchronize their displays with whatever file you are editing at any moment. It won't make much of a difference now, but once you're working on complex projects, this makes it easy for you to run test commands in the correct location.

Load and Main Loop

Once you've configured Geany, coding can begin. Before coding dice rolls as you did in the first iteration of the game, there's some setup to make this a graphical game. First, you need the libraries to let Lua produce graphics. There are a few different libraries that could be used for this, because there are several GUI frameworks that provide Lua *hooks*. However, you are specifically looking to make games, and conveniently there are game engines that can be controlled by Lua scripts. Just as Lua itself has built-in functions for common tasks, such as `math.random`, game engines have functions for common game tasks, such as a window that can go full-screen on demand, listeners for joystick and mouse input, physics, and so on.

The LÖVE engine is a game framework written specifically for Lua. Normally, you install it with either dnfdragora or the `dnf` command in a terminal, but to get the very latest version of LÖVE with all of its newest features, you should install using the `.rpm` file included with the code for this book or from `klaatu.fedorapeople.org/love-99f37ac-1.fc27.armv7hl.rpm`. An RPM file is an installer file for Linux. It's the same kind of file stored on application servers (or *repositories* in Linux terminology), but can also be downloaded directly in a web browser. You use the same command as you used to install Geany to install an RPM you have downloaded, providing the path to the file you want to install.

```
$ sudo dnf install ~/Downloads/love-99f37ac-1.fc27.
armv7hl.rpm
```

The installer asks you for permission to install several libraries that LÖVE depends upon. Accept and wait for the install to finish, which returns you to the usual prompt ($).

Writing Lua Code with LÖVE

LÖVE is a set of libraries for Lua, so it isn't an application you launch to write code. Instead, you use LÖVE functions in your code.

If Geany isn't still running, launch it now. Go to the File menu and select New. This creates an empty untitled file in your workspace. Select File ➤ Save As to save this file as `main.lua` in your `dice` project directory.

First, create two variables to set the window size for your game. This is a simple dice game and the Pi isn't a very powerful computer, so keep the window size small. At the very top of your file, type this:

```
view_w = 777
view_h = 472
```

Creating variables for the size of the window doesn't do anything special. These are normal variables containing normal numbers. It's how the game script uses these variables that actually sets the window size.

The LÖVE game engine is programmed to do just two things automatically when it's launched: call the love.load() function once, and then call the love.draw() function until the user quits. So for LÖVE to do anything with your game, you need to create both of those functions. LÖVE doesn't care what's in those functions; in fact, it expects you to fill that in yourself. In other words, it's in these functions that the actual game code goes.

Make your game code look like this:

```
view_w = 777
view_h = 472

function love.load()
-- loads once at launch
end

function love.draw()
-- main loop
end
```

Notice that functions in Lua end with the keyword end. The text now within each function block is called a *comment*, which is a line of code that the computer ignores. They're just notes for the programmer.

```
-- in Lua, this is a comment
```

29

You've already used functions in Lua, but this time you are creating your own. A function in programming is a block of self-contained code that optionally accepts input and optionally renders data as output. You'll also hear them called *methods* or even *algorithms*, but it's all the same concept: you're writing instructions for a computer, and by wrapping those instructions in a named *function*, you allow your program to use and reuse those instructions as often and whenever needed.

Spawning a window for your game is a one-time task. When the user launches your game, the window's attributes—like the size, title, and background color—only need to happen once. After those attributes are set, LÖVE can move on to the rest of the code. This means, of course, that window setup should happen in the love.load() function.

Add this to your game code:

```
function love.load()
    -- loads once at launch
    love.window.setMode(view_w,view_h,{resizable=false,
    vsync=false})
    love.window.setTitle('DiCE')
    love.graphics.setBackgroundColor(0,0,0)
end
```

It's customary to indent code blocks to signify a kind of lineage. For instance, everything is indented after function love.load() to demonstrate that the lines of code are inside that function. The word end is not indented, and closes the function. In some programming languages, like Python, this is required, but in Lua, it's entirely optional. Lua doesn't use indentation to determine programming logic; it's just a visual convention for programmers.

Most of the names of the functions are pretty descriptive, so you can probably surmise what they do. love.window.setMode sets the width and height of the window by using the variables view_w for width and view_h for height.

The `love.window.setTitle` function sets the title in the window's title bar. `love.graphics.setBackgroundColor` sets the background of the window to the RGB value 0,0,0 (black).

It's not much to look at, but you can launch your game as is. To see what you've created so far, first save your file. If you don't remember to save before previewing your game, you won't see your changes, so get used to saving often.

After your changes are saved, click the terminal tab in the bottom left of the Geany window. The bottom panel of Geany now gives you a shell prompt. The working directory in the terminal is already set to your project folder. If it isn't, change to that directory now (and check your Geany configuration later, as described earlier in this chapter).

```
$ cd ~/dice
```

The `cd` command stands for *change directory*. The ~ symbol is shorthand for *your home directory*.

From within the `dice` directory, start LÖVE, pointing it to your current directory. In Linux, your current position in the shell is represented by a dot.

```
$ love .
```

An empty window appears. Notice that its title is DiCE.

Close the window once your excitement has subsided. For this second iteration of the dice game, don't worry about how the game looks, just focus on the code. Making the game look good happens in the next iteration.

Game Code

You know from the previous version of the dice game that there are three events that must happen for the game to work. The computer must roll die, the player must roll die, and then the values of the roll must be revealed.

This process is familiar to you. There's nothing specific to LÖVE here, this is plain old Lua. Add die rolling to the code (the first and last lines are already in your code, but are here for context).

```
love.graphics.setBackgroundColor(0,0,0) --context
math.randomseed(os.time())
player = math.random(1,20)
computer = math.random(1,20)
end --for context
```

In the previous version of the game, it was up to the user to compare the rolls and to determine who had won. This time, let Lua compare the values and determine the winner. To do that, you must use two of the most common logic tools in programming: math operators and an if/then statement.

This will not work, but it's a good lesson, so add this to your code. The first line is for context.

```
computer = math.random(1,20) --for context
love.graphics.setColor(1,1,1)
if player > computer then
    love.graphics.printf("Player wins!", 0,
    view_h*0.5,view_w*0.5, 'center')
print("Player wins!")
else
    love.graphics.printf("Computer wins!", 0,
    view_h*0.5,view_w*0.5, 'center')
print("Computer wins!")
end
```

An if/then conditional statement does exactly what an if/then statement does when you use one in everyday speech. If *one* thing is true, then do *one* thing; otherwise, do *something* else. In this example, the if/then statement hinges upon whether or not the contents of the player variable is greater than the contents of the computer variable. It would be equally effective if it depended upon computer being less than player.

From the LÖVE library, the code uses the graphics.setColor function to set the foreground color and the graphics.printf to print text on the screen. Just as the standard Lua print function requires a parameter— specifically *what* to print, the love.graphics.printf function requires several parameters: what to print, when to wrap text to the next line, the location along the X and Y axes, and text justification. These parameters must be given in the order specified by the function's documentation, located at love2d.org/wiki/love.graphics.printf.

Try your game to see what happens.

```
$ love .
```

The game window opens, but it's still just a blank window. This makes it seem like your game doesn't work, but if you look at the terminal, assuming you launched the game in Geany, then you see that Lua did print a winner to your standard output. So the underlying game logic is sound.

The problem, in fact, is that your game's text was written to the screen but only persisted for a millisecond or so. The love.load() function is only called once per launch, but a screen is refreshed constantly and at a rate much faster than your eye can detect. To generate graphics that are refreshed for as long as the game is running, use the love.draw() function.

Update your code to match this:

```
computer = math.random(1,20) --for context
end --for context

function love.draw()
    love.graphics.setColor(1,1,1)
```

```
        if player > computer then
            love.graphics.printf("Player wins!", 0,
            view_h*0.5,view_w*0.5, 'center')
        print("Player wins!")
        else
            love.graphics.printf("Computer wins!", 0,
            view_h*0.5,view_w*0.5, 'center')
        print("Computer wins!")
        end
    end
```

Try your game again.

```
$ love .
```

This time, the winner is printed to the graphical game screen. The message also prints infinitely in your terminal, which provides you with some insight about why the text remains visible in the game window. The message isn't just being written once, but several times as your screen refreshes.

Graphics

There are a few problems with the game in its current state. First, it isn't very interactive. A player isn't likely to feel that they're rolling the die, virtual or otherwise, because the game just launches and declares a winner. In a related issue, there's no way to roll again except by closing the game and launching it again. And finally, the game isn't much to look at. It has no graphics, the font it uses is boring, and there's nothing that visually suggests that this humble application is a game.

To incorporate graphics and an attractive font, you must have graphics and a font to not only use but that you're permitted to ship with your game when you distribute it. You probably aren't going to distribute this first dice game that you make, but it's a good habit to get familiar with the three kinds of assets that you can use in your games: original, Creative Commons, and commissioned. The latter is art that you have someone else make for you, with the express permission granted for you to use the artwork in your game. Creative Commons is the same, in principle; someone else makes art, posts it to the Internet along with some level of permission for you to reuse it (usually you are required, at least, to give them credit for their work, which seems only fair). Failing those resources, you can just make your own artwork.

For the sake of brevity, take a look at OpenClipArt.org, a website full of Creative Commons artwork. You can search for dice and find several results, but to roll dice and show the result, you need one image per side of dice. To simplify the effort, this example uses six-sided dice instead of twenty. To make the game look a little more high-tech than it actually is, this example eschews traditional dice and instead uses a two-dimensional design. Traditional dice would be very familiar, but the results would be immediately obvious. Since there's not that much going on in this game, using a non-traditional representation of a dice roll forces an unsuspecting user to solve a little puzzle to figure out why the player or the computer wins with each roll. In other words, the game adds a game to the game. If you don't care for something so esoteric, use any graphic you like, as long as you name your image files to match those used in the example code in this book.

Fonts

Fonts have the same requirements as graphics. To use them in your game, you have to send the font file along with your game, and to do that legally, you must respect the license of whatever font you choose. You might not think about it often, but the default fonts on Windows and Apple computers are mostly owned by Microsoft, Apple, Adobe, or other companies. You're allowed to use them, but not necessarily to redistribute or sell them. Luckily, there are plenty of free and open source fonts available online.

Fonts don't often use a Creative Commons license, but have their own special Open Font License or GNU General Public License, or similar. There are several good sites offering fonts. This example uses the boldly futuristic font Orbitron from TheLeagueOfMoveableType.com. It is a good source of openly licensed fonts but does not have so many options as to be overwhelming.

Create two new directories in your `dice` folder: one called `font` and the other called `img`. To create a new directory, right-click your `dice` folder and select New ➤ Folder.

The following creates the new directories from the terminal:

```
$ mkdir ~/dice/{img,font}
```

Download the dice graphics as PNG files and also download the font. Place the dice graphic files in the `img` directory and the font TTF and LICENSE files in the `font` directory.

Graphics from OpenClipArt.org do not require attribution, so you do not have to credit the creator. Obligation is one thing and being a good sport is another, so create a new file in Geany called CREDIT. Open the file and list the assets that you are using.

```
Dice graphics by Orsonj
https://openclipart.org/detail/117277/digital-die-0

Font by the League of Moveable Type
https://www.theleagueofmoveabletype.com
```

Tables

In the current iteration of the game, the `computer` and `player` variables contain one piece of information each. The new iteration, like probably any game you create from this point, is more complex. One attribute per "object" in your program is not enough. For instance, the `player` in your game must contain a number representing its dice roll as well as a graphic that shows your user what that roll was. That's at least two data for one variable. Surely, that's not possible!

Of course, Lua has a way to make this possible. Lua uses tables to store a list of variables along with what those variables contain. At the very top of your file, create two new tables, one for each player.

```
human = {}
comp = {}
```

The tables don't contain variables yet, but you can add them as needed. For instance, give each player a name in the love.load function. The first three lines are for context.

```
math.randomseed(os.time()) --for context
computer = math.random(1,20) --for context
player = math.random(1,20) --for context
player.name = "You"
comp.name = "Computer"
```

You can also set the graphic of each player to a neutral position. In terms of the digital die graphic used in this example, neutral is die position 0.

```
player.img = love.graphics.newImage('img/d0.png')
comp.img = love.graphics.newImage('img/d0.png')
```

You also need some useful variables outside of the players. For instance, set the font for the game.

```
font = love.graphics.setNewFont("font/orbitron-bold-
webfont.ttf",72)
```

The font size is set to 72 points. That will be important later.

CHAPTER 2   SCRIPTING WITH LÖVE

Game and GUI Logic

When you were running your dice game from the Lua shell, everything was instantaneous. Applications with graphical user interfaces, by nature, tend to sit idly until the user tells it to do something. Currently, your GUI dice game launches, rolls the dice, and announces a winner. You need to slow it down so that it waits for the user before taking action.

Common conventions for making a GUI application do something are buttons and menus. Both of these are usually triggered by a mouse click. Why not make the dice game wait to roll die until the user clicks the mouse? The act of clicking the game screen helps the user feel that they have more involvement with the game, and also makes the game something that can be played several times without having to be closed and the reopened.

You already know that the main loop of a LÖVE game is the love.draw function, so that's the part of your code that you need to control. The first task is to force love.draw to wait for input before displaying any change. A common trick for such control is to create a variable and then force the main loop to wait for that variable to change before taking action.

For this game, use a variable called start, set to true, to indicate that a new game has been launched, but that the main loop is waiting for input from the user. Create the variable in love.load so that the game begins in the start mode.

```
start = true
```

Erase whatever you have in the love.draw function, replacing it with a conditional statement that checks whether start is true or not. If it is not true, then the game commences. If true, it draws the neutral die graphic.

There's quite a bit of math involved in positioning the graphics. You originally set the game window sizes in the global variables cw (canvas width) and ch (canvas height), so you know the area you have to work with.

In most computer graphic applications, LÖVE included, the upper-left corner of the canvas is 0, and the X and Y axes increase to the right and down screen (see Figure 2-7).

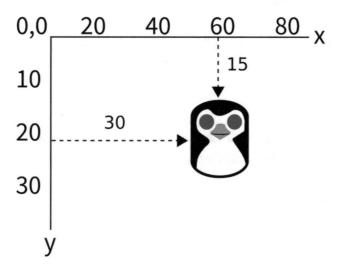

Figure 2-7. *Screen coordinates*

Technically, you could start the first dice display at 0, but so that it's not crowded against the left window edge, the example code indents it by 33 pixels. The same holds true for the distance from the top edge, which is indented by 30 pixels. The offset of the dice are set to 0, and the scale is set to 0.2, because the source graphics are larger than the screen.

The dice display on the right of the screen is slightly different. To determine its position along the X axis, the width of the canvas is divided in half (or multiplied by 0.5, as the case may be). You could do that math yourself, and then put in the number manually (777*0.5=388), but if you ever changed the canvas size, you'd have to go through your code and find all the wrong numbers and recalculate. Well, that's exactly what computers are for, so it's much smarter to take the time to figure out the correct equation rather than doing the math yourself.

```
function love.draw()
    love.graphics.setColor(1,1,1)
    if start == false then
    -- do something here
    end
    love.graphics.draw(human.img,33,30,0,0.2,0.2)
    love.graphics.draw(computer.img,cw*0.5,30,0,
    0.2,0.2)
    end
```

Save and then launch the game. At the very least, it shows you the neutral positions of the die. Not terribly exciting, but it's a good start.

Mouse Click

One of the nice things about using a game engine is that there's a lot of code already written for you. Listening and processing mouse events is a perfect example of that. Imagine having to write the code to monitor the system for mouse clicks, especially given that different operating systems and platforms send mouse click events differently. LÖVE takes care of all of that for you.

Interestingly, it's technically not the mouse *click* that you want, but the mouse release. If you set your game to start its main loop when a mouse is clicked, then it might get very confused if a user clicks and holds the button down for 10 seconds before releasing. A release, on the other hand, only happens once. To start the game when the mouse button is released, set the start variable to false.

Add this function at the bottom of your code:

```
function love.mousereleased()
start = false
end
```

It's when the mouse button is released that the dice are actually rolled, so instead of putting the dice rolls in love.load, that dice rolls must happen in the love.mousereleased function. Remove these lines from love.load:

```
player = math.random(1,20)
computer = math.random(1,20)
```

And add dice rolls to the love.mousereleased function, storing the result in the appropriate human or computer table. After the rolls happen, change the graphic in the img variable of each player to the corresponding dice image.

To tell LÖVE which image to use, you must construct the full image name using the number contained in the roll variable. You join strings together in Lua with two dots; for example, if the comp.roll variable contains 3, then 'img/comp-die'..comp.roll..'.png' translates to img/comp-die3.png.

Here's the relevant code:

```
start = false
comp.roll = math.random(1,6)
human.roll = math.random(1,6)
-- set graphics
human.img = love.graphics.newImage('img/die'..human.roll..'.png')
comp.img = love.graphics.newImage('img/comp-die'..comp.roll..'.png')
```

Winner and Loser

To drive home the point, your game should declare a winner. This logic happens in the love.mousereleased function, since it only needs to happen when the mouse button is released. Add this conditional statement to the bottom of your code, and then close the love.mousereleased function.

41

```
   if human.roll > comp.roll then
     human.win = true
   else
     human.win = false
   end
 end
```

With all the important variables set depending on how the dice roll, the main loop has relatively little to do in terms of logic. However, the main loop is still important to keep the graphics going, so now it's time to make sure that the interface responds appropriately to input.

You've already set the main loop to appear dormant until it receives input from the user, but it should also react once a mouse button is released. Specifically, it should look at the variables of the players to determine who has won the roll and announce the winner.

Insert another conditional statement in the main loop that checks for a winner. Announce the winner by printing a message to the screen using the love.graphics.printf function. To help differentiate between the human user and the computer, this example changes the foreground color to either green or red when writing the font to screen, and then back to white for general-purpose drawing.

Note   If you fail to reset the color to white, your other graphic elements may be rendered incorrectly.

You can choose whatever color you prefer. If you don't think in RGB colors, use a color picker online. Traditionally, RGB values use 0 as empty and 255 as full, but LÖVE uses 0 as black and 1 as white, with all shades in between being a decimal value. You can convert from a 0–255 value to a decimal value by dividing by 255. For example, a color picker value of (188,54,0) is (188/255,54/255,0/255) or (0.73,0.21,0).

Determining the correct position of the text and graphics also takes a little bit of math. Notice that the cw (canvas width) and ch (canvas height) variables are used to create a sort of invisible "text box" that is as wide as the canvas and that extends all the way down the canvas height *minus* 76 pixels. Why 76 pixels? Because the font was set to 72 points in the love.load function, so taking the height of the canvas minus the size of the font ensures that the text is printed, more or less, along the bottom border of the window.

```
if start == false then
  if human.win == true then
    love.graphics.setColor(0.2,1,0.2)
    love.graphics.printf("human wins!", 0, ch-76,
    cw, 'center')
    love.graphics.setColor(1,1,1)
  else
    love.graphics.setColor(1,0.2,0.2)
    love.graphics.printf("Computer wins!", 0, ch-76,
    cw, 'center')
    love.graphics.setColor(1,1,1)
  end
```

Try your game now. It responds to your click, changes the dice graphics, and announces a winner. What more could a user possibly want?

Well, since there's no visual cue for the user that the game is waiting for a mouse click and hasn't just crashed, it would be better user interface (UI) design to provide guidance for a new user. This can be implemented as an alternative to the start condition. If start is true, then that means the user has just started the game and has not yet clicked the mouse button (if the button had been clicked, the screen would display the winner and start would be set to false).

Add a friendly start message. The first three lines are for context.

```
    love.graphics.printf("Computer wins!", 0, ch-76,cw, 'center')
    love.graphics.setColor(1,1,1)
end
else
-- start message
    love.graphics.printf("Click to roll", 0, ch-76,cw, 'center')
end
```

Packaging

You now have a fully functional dice-rolling game. It's simple, but it's only about 50 lines of code and demonstrates many important principles of game logic, UI design, and programming fundamentals.

It's programmed in LÖVE, so any of your friends or family can play it as long as they install LÖVE on their platform. However, if you send them a folder of code, images, and fonts, they won't know what to do with it. It's time to package your game for distribution.

LÖVE files are nothing more than ZIP files with a special suffix, so redistributable LÖVE games are remarkably easy to build. In a terminal (you can use the one in Geany or you can launch a separate terminal window), use the zip command to bundle up the main.lua file, the font directory, and the img directory into a game file called dice.love.

```
$ cd ~/dice
$ zip dice.love -r main.lua font img
```

Open a desktop window to your dice folder and double-click dice. love. Your game launches just like any normal application would. You can send this file to anyone you want to, and as long as they install LÖVE, they can play your game.

Homework

The love.mousereleased function accepts three parameters from your operating system: the X and Y coordinates on which the mouse was clicked and the button that was released.

Try these hacks:

- The game doesn't account for a tie game. There are at least two ways to deal with a tie; try changing the code to acknowledge when the player and computer roll the same result.

- Create a version of the game that only responds to a left-click (button 1).

- Add a cheat to the game such that the computer automatically wins if the right mouse button (button 2) is released, and the player automatically wins if the middle button (button 3) is released.

- If you are feeling particularly brave, try this advanced exercise: change which dice display represents the player depending on which side of the screen the player clicks to roll.

CHAPTER 3

Modular Programming with LÖVE

The dice game in Chapter 2 was created in one file. Small programs, usually called *scripts*, are often only one file, but the larger an application gets, the less convenient it is to write it all in one monolithic file. After all, most large applications aren't written by just one developer but a whole team, and only one person can work on a file at a time. Game engines are pieces in a modular system, since the engine is useless to users without a game. Additionally, if you keep your code modular, you might be able to reuse a file from one project in the next project.

In this chapter, you set up a typical project directory and program a modular Blackjack game using a custom card dealer library (see Figure 3-1). The game allows a player to click an empty deck of cards to draw a card and compete against the computer in an effort to get as close to 21 without exceeding it. When the player decides to stop drawing new cards for fear of exceeding 21, the player clicks the game table to signal that their hand is complete. The game keeps a running total of card values, and detects and announces a winner. The player may click the deck again to start a new game.

© Seth Kenlon 2019
S. Kenlon, *Developing Games on the Raspberry Pi*,
https://doi.org/10.1007/978-1-4842-4170-7_3

Figure 3-1. The card game you're about to make with Lua

Project Directory

There is no rule for how you organize your code, but there is a general convention, especially within the open source software world. You can get a feel for this convention if you browse a few open source projects online, and you've already implemented some principles as you created your dice game.

First, your code should have its own directory. You already have a directory called dice in your home folder, so create one for your new game. You can make a new directory from your Enlightenment desktop or in a terminal.

```
$ mkdir ~/blackjack
```

For your dice game, you created directories for images and fonts, so create those directories in your new project directory.

```
$ mkdir ~/blackjack/img
    $ mkdir ~/blackjack/font
```

One of the primary goals of this project is to learn to use more than one file of Lua code. Your project directory would get pretty untidy if you kept all of your code files in the main folder, so make a directory for your source code. It's common for source code to be kept in a directory called src.

```
$ mkdir ~/blackjack/src
```

That takes care of the obvious folders, but there are also a few files that most people expect to find in a software source directory: README and LICENSE.

A README file tells a casual observer what your project is, what code it contains, and so on. You can create the file now and fill it in later. Give it the .md extension to help online hosting services recognize it as documentation.

```
$ mkdir ~/blackjack/README.md
```

The LICENSE file tells anyone looking at your source how they may use your code. There are several varieties of open source licenses, listed in detail at gnu.org/licenses/license-list.html.

As the author of the code, I license the program that you are about to copy and learn from under the GNU Public License version 3 (GPLv3). This grants you permission to redistribute, or even sell, and modify it as you wish, as long as you give everyone else permission to do the same. As open source licenses go, this is a common and sensible agreement: you get to do whatever you want to do with the code as long as you let the next person in line do whatever they want.

Many popular open source licenses are aggregated for convenient download at https://gitlab.com/everylicense/everylicense. As a developer, you use a license every time you start a project, so you may as well have the common ones handy. Since the everylicense project is kept as a Git repository, the process of downloading and keeping it updated is best done with Git, which you installed while setting up your developer environment. The act of downloading a Git project (or *repository* in Git terminology) from the Internet to your computer is called making a clone. In this command, the \ character allows you to type one command on several lines. If your terminal automatically wraps your text (most do), then you don't have to type the \ character (but it won't hurt if you do).

```
$ git clone \
https://gitlab.com/everylicense/everylicense.git \
~/everylicense.clone
```

Copy the GNU Public License version 3 from the everylicense directory into your code directory, and then rename it LICENSE. You know how to do this in your graphical file manager, but you can do it all in one step from a terminal.

```
$ cp ~/everylicense.git/gnu_gpl_3/gpl-3.0.txt ~/blackjack/LICENSE
```

That takes care of all the bureaucracy and preparation. Now you need to build a virtual card deck.

Classes and Objects

In the dice game, you had two dice "objects" to code. An object in code is a little bit like a mold in real life: the code defines the basic properties of an object, and usually allows customization, as needed. Object-oriented programming (OOP) is the prevailing means of developing software today, so learning to structure your code into objects is important, and by the end of this book, it's something you'll do naturally.

For the dice game, you coded each object separately because there were only two die. This time, you are writing a game involving 52 playing cards, so it doesn't make sense to code each card separately, just as programmers in major game studios don't manually code every single enemy you have to fight.

When a program requires lots of different objects with basically the same properties, you can use a `class`. A class is a snippet of code—usually stored in its own unique file—that your main program uses as a template when building an object in your game. This template not only generates an object for your program, it creates a whole infrastructure with variables and other properties unique to that one instance of the object.

Open Geany and create a new, empty file called `card.lua`. Technically, Lua doesn't have classes, but it has tables that can be treated like classes. You've already created a table for the dice game, so some of this process may seem familiar to you.

First, establish a table called `Card` to represent a single card in a deck. In this case, the table can be empty.

```
Card = {}
```

Next, create a function called `Card.init` (the word `init` is a common programming term meaning *initialize* or *create*). For the dice game, you used functions, such as `math.random()` and `love.load()`, included in Lua. This time, you are creating your own function.

The same way the `math.random` function requires numbers as arguments, your `Card` function needs to know what kind of card to create. Since that is expected to be different each time you create a card, you use variables to represent them in this template.

```
function Card.init(suit,value)
    local self = setmetatable({}, Card)
    self.suit = suit
    self.value = value
    return self
end
```

In this `Card.init` function, you establish a local variable called `self`, which uses a special Lua extension called a `metatable`, as a kind of container for all the properties about that individual instance of a card. A card's `self` variable ensures that each card can keep track of whatever makes it unique.

Since each card created gets unique memory out of your computer's RAM, each one can track properties such as its suit and value. At the end of the creation process, the `Card` class alerts your main program of its `self` data, which you can use in your game.

Save the `card.lua` file and create a new one called `main.lua`.

A Lua program knows where to look for the standard Lua functions, but Lua doesn't know anything about your own custom `Card` class. So that you can use your custom function, you use the `require` keyword.

```lua
require("card")
```

This prompts Lua to search the current directory for a library called card.

To create a card using your function, create a new variable and invoke your function, along with two arguments: one for the suit you want your new card to belong to and one for the face value.

Since this is just a simple example, you won't see your card on screen, so use Lua's `print` function to print the specifics about the card you have just created.

```lua
local card = Card.init("hearts",8)

print(card.suit)
print(card.value)
```

Use the terminal at the bottom of the Geany interface to run the program.

```
$ cd ~/blackjack
$ lua ./main.lua
hearts
8
```

Try adding some more cards, and then print the results.

```
local card0 = Card.init("hearts",8)
local card1 = Card.init("diamonds",2)
local card2 = Card.init("spades",6)

print(card0.suit .. " " .. card0.value)
print(card0.suit .. " " .. card1.value)
print(card0.suit .. " " .. card2.value)
$ lua ./main.lua
hearts 8
diamonds 2
spades 6
```

Your class produces, upon request, a card "object." It's not a physical object, but it's a virtual playing card with unique properties from the next. Each "object" is produced by filling a variable with a table containing preset variables that you have defined as an inherent attribute of the object. This is an important principle in modern programming because it lets you make templates for constructs in your program that you want to use over and over again.

Randomized Cards

Now that you have a card-producing Lua library, you must use it in a way that is useful in a game of Blackjack.

Blackjack is a simple game of chance and calculated risk. Each player draws a card and adds it to their hand until they are as close to 21 as possible. When both players are satisfied, they compare their hands. The player closest to 21 wins. If a player goes over 21, they lose.

It's important for Blackjack to be random. Your dice game also used random numbers, so you know that when producing a random number, you constrain Lua with a minimum and a maximum value. But Lua has no knowledge of playing cards, so you can't just tell it to randomly pick a suit or a face card. However, you can create a table listing each suit and a table listing each possible face value and then tell the computer to pick from those numbered lists.

Change your main.lua file so that it matches this simple LÖVE project:

```lua
require("card")

WIDE = 900
HIGH = 600
suits  = { "hearts","spades","clubs","diamonds" }
values = { "Ace","2","3","4","5","6","7","8","9","10","Jack",
"Queen","King" }
hand   = {} -- player hand
total  = 0  -- player score
comp   = {} -- computer hand
ai     = 0  -- computer score

love.window.setTitle(' Blackjack ')
love.window.setMode( WIDE,HIGH )

function love.load()
end

function love.draw()
end
```

This sets up a LÖVE window, an empty table to represent the player and their computer opponent, and a basic skeleton for your code.

This also creates two tables containing card data. Like many languages, Lua can extract an item from a list by number (although unlike many languages, Lua starts counting a list at 1 rather than 0). You can see this at work by launching a Lua shell in a terminal either in the lower pane of Geany or elsewhere on your system.

```
$ lua
> suits = { "hearts","diamonds","spades","clubs" }
> print(suits[1])
hearts
> print(suits[4])
clubs
```

You can also analyze the table itself. For instance, with the # symbol, you can see the number of items that are in the table.

```
> print(#suits)
4
```

You can also add items to the end of a table.

```
> suits[5] = "joker"
> print(suits[5])
joker
```

Since you already know how to get a random value from Lua, you can use your card generator library to produce a card object with a random suit and value.

There are a lot of drawing cards in Blackjack, and there are two players that need cards. If you tried to write the code for a new card every time your game needs to generate a card, you'd end up with hundreds of lines of inefficient code. What your program needs is a card generation function that you can call whenever a new card is required. At the very bottom of your file, enter this code:

```
function cardgen()
    local c = math.random(1,4)
    local s = suits[c]
    local c = math.random(1,13)
    local v = values[c]
    card = Card.init(s,v)
    return card
end
```

To use the random function, you must initiate a random seed, so change your love.load() function to

```
function love.load()
    math.randomseed(os.time())
end
```

This function creates a temporary variable called c and gives it a random number between 1 and 4. Then it creates another temporary variable called s and uses c to select one item from the suits table. It does basically the same thing with the values table for a variable called v, and then it calls your card generator library to create a new card with whatever random results are in the s and v variables.

At the end of the function, there is a return statement. This means that after the function runs, it outputs information, which can be assigned to a variable.

If a player draws a card, then the player also needs a hand where those cards can be placed. That's what the empty player and comp tables are for. Add this to the bottom of your file:

```
function love.mousereleased(x,y,button)
```

```
    if button == 1 then
        var = cardgen()
        hand[#hand+1]=var
        total = total+var.value
    end
end
```

Like your dice game, user interaction is a simple mouse click. The mousereleased function of LÖVE sends a variety of information, including where on the screen the mouse was released, and which physical button on the mouse was released. You don't have to use the information, but it lets you be precise about what input you want your game to respond to.

In this code, the left mouse button triggers the creation of a new card object by creating a variable called var, which is assigned the output of your card generator function. Your card generator function, of course, calls your card library so that var contains a table detailing the suit and value of a card.

Once the card has been created, the var variable containing the card is copied into the player's hand. When you add an item to a table, you must add it to the end of the list; so to specify where in the table the new card goes, you use the #hand shorthand to get the current length of the table plus 1.

After the card has been added to the player's hand, tally up the current total score for the player. The value of each card is contained in the card's table. The current card is still going by the name var, so you add whatever is contained in total to var.value.

There are still no graphics being drawn, so add some text to help you see that your application is working up to this point. You can use whatever font you want, but this sample code uses Ostrich from TheLeagueofMoveableType.com.

Note   As a courtesy to the person who created the font you use, credit the font in your README file.

```
function love.load()
    math.randomseed(os.time())
    font = love.graphics.setNewFont("font/ostrich-sans-
    regular.ttf",72)
    love.graphics.setColor(1,1,1)
end
```

To print the card and total score on screen, you must loop over each card in the player's hand table. For each entry in a table, there are technically at least two values: an index number and the actual entry. Lua's ipairs function unpacks a table for you, placing each pair into two variables of your choice.

```
function love.draw()
    for i, card in ipairs(hand) do
        love.graphics.clear()
        love.graphics.printf(card.suit .. " " .. total, 0,
        HIGH-76,WIDE, 'center')
    end
end
```

At this point, the application runs, but there's a serious bug. Launch it and see if you encounter the bug. Better still, see if you can identify the problem.

```
$ cd ~/blackjack/
$ love .
```

The problem lies in how the cards are scored. Some cards are listed as numbers, but others are face cards. Lua can't very well add "Jack" to the total score, so it crashes.

The obvious solution to this problem is to change the King, Queen, and Jack values to 10, and the Ace value to 1. However, if the King and Queen and Jack are all changed to 10, there's no way to tell them apart when randomly choosing which to display.

So instead, create a function to process the cards' values. In this sample, the value passed to the function becomes c while being processed. That means that when you call the function, it requires an argument. Add this to the bottom of your file:

```
function face(c)
    if c == "Jack"
    or c == "King"
    or c == "Queen" then
        val=10
    elseif c == "Ace" then
    val=1
    else
    val=tonumber(c)
    end
    return val
end
```

Use this function before adding the value of a card to the total score so that you are no longer trying to do mathematics on words and numbers. Notice that when you call the face function, you pass var.value to it so that it knows what to process.

```
function love.mousereleased(x,y,button)
    if button == 1 then
        var = cardgen()
        hand[#hand+1]=var
    val = face(var.value)
    total = total+val
    end
end
```

Launch your game again. You can keep drawing cards endlessly. No bugs!

Graphics

A game of cards using names and numbers is effective, but not pretty. To make this a real people-pleasing game, you need graphics. Then again, 52 cards are a lot of graphics to come up with. Luckily, a few people on OpenClipArt.org have already done the work for you, posting them as free assets with no recompense required. Download the cards from this book's code repository, or make your own.

Note   While OpenClipArt.org requires nothing in return, it's considered good form to credit those who have helped you make a project. For this reason, you should open your README file in Geany and thank the OpenClipArt.org artists whose work you are using: mariotomo, nicubunu, and notklaatu.

Place the .png files in the img folder of your code directory. They must be named in the Value-of-suit.png format; for example, 2-of-hearts.png.

When drawing objects in a window, it's typically useful to establish variables for padding and scale. These both act as an easy, standard location to make global changes in the event that your screen size changes or you start running out of room. Add these variables to the top of your file (the first two lines are for context):

```
WIDE = 900
HIGH = 600
pad   = WIDE*0.04
scale = 0.66
```

When your game uses your card library to generate a new card, it can use these graphics as the card's visual representation. For that to work, though, your card library must have a space in its table to hold a reference to the appropriate graphic. You did this sort of assignment in your dice game. Open card.lua and change it to look like this:

```lua
Card = { }

function Card.init(suit,value)
    local self = setmetatable({}, Card)
    self.suit = suit
    self.value = value
    self.img = love.graphics.newImage( "img/" .. self.value ..
    "-of-" .. self.suit .. ".png")
    return self
end
```

Now whenever a new card is created, the card object is assigned a graphic with a filename corresponding to its randomly selected suit and name.

Start with the easy graphic first: the one that doesn't change. The deck from which a player draws new cards is represented by the back of a playing card. This virtual deck sits in the upper-right corner of the game screen, serving as a visual cue for the player, as well as an actual button. To render this graphic, you must generate a card object for it using your card library; but since it's only needed once, you create it in the love.load() function.

```lua
function love.load()
    math.randomseed(os.time())
    playback= Card.init("card","back")          -- create a deck
                                                    graphic
    slot = playback.img:getWidth()*scale        -- calculate
                                                    card sizes
    love.graphics.setBackgroundColor(0.3,0.5,0.3) -- green
```

```
    font = love.graphics.setNewFont("font/ostrich-sans-
    regular.ttf",72)
    love.graphics.setColor(1,1,1)
end
```

Since your game will draw multiple cards on the screen, it's helpful
to have a variable representing the size of a virtual card. In the preceding
code, the slot variable is assigned to the results of the getWidth function
performed on the playback card multiplied by the current scale. This
allows you to use slot to represent any space occupied by a card. In the
real world, you would use inches or centimeters, but those don't mean
much on screens, so for this game, you use slot instead.

In addition to creating the deck and a variable for one unit of card
measure, this code sample sets the background of the game window to
green.

Next, draw the card deck and some instructions for the player using
your new padding and scale variables to control placement. Additionally,
instead of just rendering text describing the cards that the player has
drawn, you can draw the actual cards by looping through the hand table
and drawing whatever image is assigned to each entry.

```
function love.draw()
    love.graphics.printf("Click deck to deal.",pad,66,
    WIDE,'left')
    love.graphics.printf("Click anywhere to hold.",pad,122,
    WIDE,'left')
    love.graphics.draw(playback.img,WIDE-slot-pad,pad,0,scale,
    scale,0,0)
    for i, card in ipairs(hand) do
        love.graphics.draw(card.img,pad*i,pad*i,0,scale,scale,0,0)
    end
end
```

The instructions state that a player must click the card deck to draw a card, and click anywhere else to *hold*, which is Blackjack jargon for not drawing any more cards. So instead of accepting any click as a draw action, limit the "hot" area of the screen to just the location of the deck. To do this, you analyze the X and Y coordinates of each click, which is sent to you automatically by LÖVE's mousereleased function.

```
function love.mousereleased(x,y,button)
    if button == 1
    and x > WIDE-slot-pad
    and y < slot*1.5 then
        var = cardgen()
        hand[#hand+1]=var
    val = face(var.value)
    total = total+val
    else
    hold = true
    end
end
```

Launch your project. The deck should appear in the upper-right corner; the instructions are on the right. If you click the green tabletop, nothing happens, but if you click the card deck, you are dealt a new card. This happens until the cards flow right off the screen.

Competition

Blackjack can be a solitaire game in real life, but people playing competitive computer games usually expect a definitive win and lose condition. That means you need to program an opponent.

According to the Internet, the prevailing opinion on Blackjack is
to hold at around 17. This being the only real "strategy" (such as it is),
programming an AI is a simple conditional: if the computer's hand is 17
or higher, then the computer must hold. To make the game a little more
exciting, you can make the computer more reckless than popular strategy
dictates by setting its hold tolerance to 16 or 15.

The AI's draw action is basically the same as the player's, except that
the computer's hand table is called comp and its score is ai.

```
function love.mousereleased(x,y,button)
    if ai < 16 then
        var = cardgen()
        var = cardgen()
        comp[#comp+1]=var
        val = face(var.value)
        ai = ai+val
        print(var.value)
    end

    if button == 1
    and x > WIDE-slot-pad
    and y < slot*1.5 then
        var = cardgen()
        hand[#hand+1]=var
        val = face(var.value)
        total = total+val
    else
        hold = true
    end
end
```

Notice that the computer takes its turn *before* the player. This means that whether or not the player is drawing a card or holding, the computer still has the opportunity to take a turn.

Drawing the computer's hand on the screen is also basically the same as drawing the player's hand. It uses a loop over the computer's hand, with a different offset so that the computer's cards aren't rendered on top of the player's. To further help the player differentiate between hands, add a tint to the computer's hand.

```
function love.draw()
    love.graphics.printf("Click deck to deal.",pad,66,WIDE, 'left')
    love.graphics.printf("Click anywhere to hold.",pad,122,WIDE,
    'left')

    for i, card in ipairs(hand) do
        love.graphics.draw(card.img,pad*i,pad*i,0,scale,scale,0,0)
    end
    for i, card in ipairs(comp) do
        love.graphics.setColor(0.7,0.8,0.7)
    love.graphics.draw(card.img,(WIDE*0.33)+(76)+(pad*i),pad*i,
    0,scale,scale,0,0)
    love.graphics.setColor(1,1,1)
    end
    love.graphics.draw(playback.img,WIDE-slot-pad,pad,0,
    scale,scale,0,0)
end
```

Just because the computer chooses to hold doesn't necessarily mean that the player is going to hold, so a hold flag can only be set by the player, which is currently the else statement in the player's mousereleased action.

Once a player chooses to hold, the game is over. At that point, you could program a pop-up box to ask if the player wants to play another hand. However, when designing an interface, it's better to default to success as often as possible. A player knows how to exit the game, so there's no reason to bother them with prompts. That means if the player has decided to hold, the game should just start over. For that to happen, you need a reset function.

For a new game to start, hands and scores must be set back to empty, and the hold flag must be cleared. Your reset function doesn't need any information and it doesn't return any data, it just clears everything out when called. Add it to the bottom of your main.lua file.

```
function reset()
    total = 0
    hand = {}
    comp = {}
    ai = 0
    hold = false
end
```

It's good practice to declare globally significant variables early, so add a hold variable set to false at the top of your file. The first two lines are for context.

```
pad   = WIDE*0.04
scale = 0.66
hold  = false
```

A reset is called when two things are true: the player has decided to hold, but the player has clicked somewhere on the screen. However, since clicking the table is also a sign to hold, some safeguards need to be introduced to prevent clicking the table from both starting a new game and signaling the end of that new game. A simple way to prevent a premature endgame signal is to ensure that the player has at least one card on the table before flagging a hold or a reset.

Change your mousereleased function to its final version.

```
function love.mousereleased(x,y,button)
    if hold == true
    and total > 1 then
        reset()
    end
    -- computer
    if ai < 16 then
        var = cardgen()
    var = cardgen()
    comp[#comp+1]=var
    val = face(var.value)
    ai = ai+val
    end

    if button == 1
    and x > WIDE-slot-pad
    and y < slot*1.5 then
    var = cardgen()
        hand[#hand+1]=var
    val = face(var.value)
    total = total+val
    elseif #hand >= 1 then
        hold = true
    end
end
```

Launch the game to verify that it's working and to see what's missing.

Winning

All that's left now is to detect and declare a winner. Sometimes, it's easier to detect failure than success, so the first thing you can do is add a watcher function to check whether or not the player has exceeded 21. If ever a player's hand exceeds 21, then there's no way for the player to win, so the `hold` flag can be set immediately to bring the game to an end.

LÖVE's `love.update(dt)` function is similar to the `love.draw()` function, except it doesn't draw anything on screen, it just runs logic code in the background.

```
function love.update(dt)
    if tonumber(total) > 21 then
        hold = true
    end
end
```

The Lua `tonumber` method is a safeguard to ensure that the content of `total` is definitely treated as a number and not a string. It's not very likely that LÖVE would get confused about that, or that `total` would contain a string, but since it's a math operation, it doesn't hurt to ensure that both sides of the equation are numbers.

Detecting a winner is a little more complex. The player wins if

- Their hand is less than or equal to 21

- But also greater than the computer's hand

- If the computer's hand is greater than 21

Furthermore,

- It's a tie if both hands are equal

- It's a bust if both hands are greater than 21

Add a winner function at the end of your file. It returns data about the winner. The if statement happens in the order it is written, so if you check only to see whether the computer's hand is more than 21, then no other condition in which that is true will ever happen.

```
function winner()
    if tonumber(total) <= 21
    and tonumber(total) > tonumber(ai) then
    win = "You"
    elseif tonumber(total) <= 21
    and tonumber(ai) == tonumber(total) then
    win = "Tie"
    elseif tonumber(ai) > 21
    and tonumber(total) > 21 then
    win = "Bust"
    elseif tonumber(ai) > 21
    and tonumber(total) <= 21 then
    win = "You"
    else
    win = "Computer"
    end
    return win
end
```

There can be no win condition unless a hold has either been chosen or imposed, so it's safe to only call the winner function if hold is true. You can check this in the love.draw() section of your code, using this as an opportunity to display on screen a running total of each hand until a winner is announced.

Add this code to the end of your `love.draw()` function, just above the final end line. The first line is for context.

```
love.graphics.draw(playback.img,WIDE-slot-pad,pad,0,scale,
scale,0,0)

if hold == false then
love.graphics.printf("You: " .. total .. " vs. Computer: "
.. ai, 0, HIGH-76,WIDE, 'center')
else
win = winner()
love.graphics.printf("Winner: " .. win .. "!!", 0,
HIGH-76,WIDE, 'center')
end
```

The game is complete. Launch it to try it out.

To distribute your new game easily, you can follow the same procedure as you did for your dice game. Zip the files and directories required to play, and then launch from the desktop.

```
$ cd ~/blackjack
$ zip blackjack.love -r main.lua card.lua font img
```

Open a desktop window to your `blackjack` folder and double-click `blackjack.love`. Your game launches just like any normal application. You can send this file to anyone you want to, and as long as they install LÖVE, they can play your game.

Homework

Here are some tasks to explore after reading this chapter.

- The computer only gets one final turn if the player holds. Introduce a second hold variable, such as `aihold`, to detect when the computer has decided to hold, regardless of what the player has done. Calculate the winner only after both the computer and the player have decided to hold.

- Ostensibly, your deck of cards should only have one of each card in it, but in the current state of the code, there is a chance that the same card could be generated twice. Can you come up with a way to ensure that once a card has been drawn, there is no chance of it being drawn again until the next round? Hint: the answer may involve another set of tables.

- The Planter application at `https://gitlab.com/planter/planter` allows you to create project directory templates so that you don't have to manually set up a project's skeleton every time you start something new. Try to install it, and then try to use it.

CHAPTER 4

Analog Programming

Now that you've gotten the feel for how programming happens on the computer, it's time to stop and consider how projects get from concept to code. In the previous chapters, this book has dictated what you programmed, and each time you ended up with exactly what the book proscribed.

In the real world, though, you have to plan what you're going to program before you sit down to write code. If you fail to do that, you generally end up with a game that's so poorly coded that you have to throw it out and start from scratch, or else it runs slowly and inefficiently. Planning reduces your time fumbling around with code and increases the time you get to spend on successful programming, graphics, sound, and other non-essential additions to your game.

The good news is that the planning process is still programming, only instead of writing code, you're using logic and mental equations to program with pen and paper. Any good system can be implemented on paper, so don't fool yourself into thinking that computers are unique. It's just as important to understand programming and game design in the physical world as it is to understand how those concepts get translated into digital bytes.

© Seth Kenlon 2019
S. Kenlon, *Developing Games on the Raspberry Pi*,
https://doi.org/10.1007/978-1-4842-4170-7_4

Game Theory

What is a game? Most of us play games in some form, but few of us stop to consider what makes a game feel like a game. You have now programmed at least two games, and if you think about what you have learned, you will likely detect a few common elements not only in what you have made but also in other games you may have played.

You might think, at first, that a game requires competition. While some games do require players to compete against one another, other games require them to work together to defeat a common threat. In some games, a player is just trying to beat his or her own best score. So in broad terms, a game requires a *win condition.*

Once a win condition is declared, it's natural to add obstacles that block players from making the win condition true. In some games, the obstacles are other players or a computer playing the part of other players. In other games, the obstacles are forces of nature, physics, or time itself.

Since most games are intended to be played more than once, the obstacles also must change from play to play. Games that don't change are predictable and eventually cease to challenge the player, which is usually considered the thing that makes games fun.

In fact, if you think about the most enduring games, there are ones that are never the same, like chess, poker, and Dungeons & Dragons, and those that have had their challenges completely redefined, as speed runners have done for Super Mario Bros. and other relatively stagnate games.

You already learned about randomness in the previous two games you made, so creating obstacles that change with each play-through is familiar to you.

The next game that you program in this book is a fantasy card game inspired by games like Magic: The Gathering, Hearthstone, Pathfinder Adventure Card Game, and other trading card games. It will teach you the concepts necessary for all kinds of games, including collision detection, saved game states, graphics, and more. But first, the game must be designed—keeping the game theory principles that you just learned in mind.

Experimental Design

Step away from your Raspberry Pi for this section. If you have a deck of playing cards, you can use that during this exercise; otherwise, find some blank index cards or a few sheets of paper cut down to approximate playing-card size.

Tip   At minimum, a game designer's toolkit should contain a deck of playing cards and some dice. Neither are items that you will necessarily use in your final version, but they both provide important templates for common game elements; the cards are quick and easy representations of different game elements, and dice produce randomness.

You're going to invent a new game that modernizes the game that you just programmed, Blackjack. Although the initial design uses a standard deck of cards as a tool, ultimately, you will style the game as a battle scenario, so the game's name is Battlejack.

There will be several iterations of this new game, and while this book proscribes much of the game to you, you are encouraged to add your own variations along the way. There are no right or wrong answers here. Any idea is worth trying. And if something breaks the game, then you can adapt it or throw it out as needed.

Iteration One

The goal in Blackjack is to be the player with cards adding up to 21, so the goal of Battlejack is the same, only in Battlejack, it's the dealer trying to get to 21 while the player attempts to prevent it. The player may cancel out a card that the dealer attempts to use in the journey to 21 with a card of an equal or greater number. For example, if the dealer puts down a 5 of clubs, the player can "kill" that card with a 5 of hearts or greater.

Each player takes a suit: the dealer is clubs, and the player is hearts. The player starts with a hand of three cards. On the player's turn, one action may be taken: either a card may be drawn from the deck, or a card may be played against the dealer. On the dealer's turn, a card from the deck is revealed and placed on the table. If the card is a club, then it counts toward the dealer's goal of 21. If it is a heart, it is discarded.

Using only the hearts and clubs from a deck of cards, try playing a hand with these rules and see how the game goes. Here's some sample play.

1. Player: draws initial hand: 2♣, 3♣, 5♣.

2. Dealer: 9♣. Total score is now 9.

3. Player: draws Ace♣.

4. Dealer: draws a 3♥, which is discarded.

5. Player: draws 7♥.

6. Dealer: draws 10♣. Total score is now 19.

7. Player: draws Ace♥.

8. Dealer: draws 8♣. Total score is now 27. Game over.

Regardless of how your own play test went, you probably see some problems with the game's current state. The central mechanic of canceling out a card with a more powerful one never even had a chance to be used, so that's a clear indication that something is amiss. The player's initial hand consisted entirely of cards from the dealer's suit, which didn't make for a very empowering start. And finally, the likelihood of the dealer reaching exactly 21 is extremely low. In Blackjack, a game can end without anyone reaching 21 because the closest one wins; but in this game, only one side is trying to reach 21, leaving no basis for comparison.

Before proceeding to the next section, take a moment to modify some of the rules and play another hand of Battlejack to see how your changes affect the game.

Iteration Two

It's obvious that the player and dealer drawing from the same deck is problematic, because it means that each side of the game ends up with cards that are useless to them. You can try to think of a solution to this yourself, but here are two suggestions.

- Instead of limiting the total deck to just two suits, use all four available suits. The player uses all red cards and the dealer uses all black cards.

- The player and the dealer get separate decks, such that the player always draws from a red deck, and the dealer always draws from a black deck.

The first option adds variety, but it doesn't actually change game play. The second option helps, but it alienates the two players from one another. Each player has a unique deck, both players know exactly what one another's deck contains, and it more or less turns into a matching game or a reverse game of Go Fish.

Another serious problem with the game is that there's actually no win condition for the player. The dealer wins by reaching 21. Since the probability of the dealer hitting exactly 21 is so low, you might loosen the constraints and declare the winner at 21 or more, but there's still no way for the player to win until the dealer runs out of cards. In effect, that does emulate a survival game, so maybe this is a path you want to explore. You could design some cards with common survival themes, such that what is now the black deck consists of various zombies and related threats, and what is now the red deck contains the usual anti-zombie measures.

But even with a cool survival game theme, the game is still very much limited to action and reaction. The game does have some randomness, because the decks are shuffled, but interestingly, the knowledge of what each deck contains lessens the effectiveness of the randomness. Even though the player doesn't know the order of the cards in the dealer's deck, the player knows exactly what it contains. When deciding which cards to "spend" to kill a black card, the player can budget using their knowledge of the enemy deck. And worse still, sometimes the order of the cards creates an unbeatable game for the player, so the player has no sense of control over the game, and the stakes are always exactly the same.

Try playing again, this time with this revised rule set.

1. Split a standard deck of cards into a red deck and a black deck. Place one Joker in each deck.

2. Take six black cards from the black deck and shuffle them into the red deck. These are, effectively, penalties that add unpredictable randomness in the player's deck.

3. The player draws three cards at the start of the game.

4. On the dealer's turn, one card from the dealer's deck is drawn and placed face up on the table. This is the dealer's "stash." When a dealer's stash adds up to 21 or more, the dealer wins.

If the player has a black card in their hand, then the
dealer compels that card from the player's hand into
the dealer's stash.

5.   On the player's turn, the player draws one card from
the player deck. There is no hand limit. If a black
card is drawn, the player must hold it; it cannot be
played or discarded.

The player may then either "stash" a card by placing
one card face up in front of them. When a player's
stash reaches 21 or more, the player wins.

Alternatively, a player may "attack" the dealer
by eliminating one card in the dealer's stash. To
eliminate a card in the dealer's stash, the player
must sacrifice one or more cards that add up to the
face value of the dealer's card. Jacks, Kings, and
Queens all count as 10, and Aces as 1.

Only one card may be eliminated per turn.

At the end of the player's turn, they draw enough
cards to bring their hand back to three.

6.   If a Joker is drawn, it destroys all cards in the dealer's
stash.

A few play tests reveal that the game is in much better shape. Even if
you can't express why, you probably find that the game feels better. It feels
better because the choices and calculations that the player has to make
are now subjective. The player has no way of knowing which six cards
from the black deck are in their own deck, so there's true randomness
in the decks at play. There are moments of surprise when a black card is
drawn. And each player's strategy is inherently different: the dealer uses

brute force, marching heedlessly onward toward 21, while the player is forced to choose on each turn whether to fight or bolster their own stash. Sometimes, a player has the perfect hand to achieve 21 but needs two turns to stash, and so must gamble that the dealer's stash, hovering though it may be at 17, won't reach 21 on the dealer's next turn.

In other words, there's some skill, there's risk, and there are some good turns of luck and some bad turns of luck. And every game is different.

Iteration Three

The game is functional now, and fun too. For the third iteration, try to think abstractly about the game. It has been designed with a standard set of playing cards, but think about your favorite genre and imagine how that might be applied to this game. Instead of just playing by numbers, the player could take the role of a barbarian chieftain battling an onslaught of orcs, or a doctor fighting the spread of a global pandemic, or a starbase captain deploying star fighters against an invading empire.

There may also be an opportunity to add more resource variety. Right now, all cards drawn by the player are cards that get stashed or played, and they are all basically the same. For a few play tests, use all red Jacks, Kings, and Queens as powerup cards: they don't count as 10, but as a +1, +2, and +3, respectively. In this version of the game, the player can beat a 9 in the dealer's stash with a 6 and a +3 Queen powerup, or a 4 with a 2 and a +2 powerup, and so on. This could potentially cause a balance problem, because now the dealer has six cards worth 10 points that the player doesn't have, but it adds flexibility to play, so it may be worth the imbalance. Try it out and see what you think.

Try out other changes of your own design, too. Some changes will break the game, making it too easy or impossible to win, but other changes will make the game uniquely yours.

Pseudo Code for Battlejack

Once you're happy with a game concept, it's time to write what's called *pseudo code*. Pseudo code is an informal but structured method of planning out a program without worrying about syntax and other details. It's purely an exercise in logic and planning. Pseudo code doesn't have to be right, it can be changed later, but it serves as a good guide for you when you sit down at a blank screen to start writing code.

By design, there are several similarities between Battlejack and Blackjack, which you have already programmed. In fact, you will reuse your card dealer library from Blackjack for Battlejack. Think about the programming tricks you know, and how they apply to Battlejack.

```
Construct a player deck and a dealer deck.

Construct a table to track which cards have already been drawn.

Construct a table to track the player's current hand,
Construct a table to track the dealer's hand.

if player[#player] < 3 then
    draw another card
end

if card dragged to stash then
    add card.val to total
elseif cards dragged to dealer_stash then
    compare player_card.val to dealer_card.val
    if player_card.val > dealer_card.val then
        remove dealer card from dealer_stash
    else
    wait for another card to be added
    end
end
```

```
if total > 21 then
    player wins
elseif ai > 21 then
    dealer wins
end
```

At just 20 lines, this is obviously a very simplified picture of what the game requires, but it's a good "big picture" view of what is needed. Having it as a guide will help you stay focused when it comes time to write the actual code.

Documentation

It's just as useful for you as a programmer, and even more useful for your players, if you document your game before you even begin writing code. In big companies, this step is typically done by the UX (user experience) team. They literally draw out what a program is intended to look like, where buttons and menus appear, and what each button or widget does. This is helpful to you while coding because you know where to put your interface elements, and it's good for your users because you can usually repurpose the design specs as user-facing documentation explaining how to play the game.

Figure 4-1 shows a sample spec for Battlejack.

When the game launches, the player is greeted with a menu screen that allows the user to resume a saved game or start a new game, adjust settings for full-screen or windowed display, and determine whether or not tutorial tips are displayed during play.

During game play, the user clicks their own deck to draw a card. During their turn, the player clicks and drags cards to either the dealer's stash to cancel out a card in play, or to their own score box to add their card to their own stash. Onscreen prompts alert the player of their choices.

If a player attempts to cancel a dealer card out with a less powerful card (trying to cancel a five-strength card with a three-strength card, for example), nothing happens. The player may add powerups or additional cards to complete the action, or click and drag the card back into their hand to continue.

There are no undo functions. Once a move has been made, the move is not retractable.

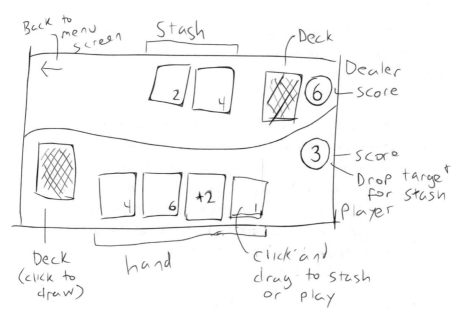

Figure 4-1. *Design spec for Battlejack*

A spec document doesn't necessarily have to be followed to the letter, but it serves as a guide and a target while coding. Some adjustments might have to be made. Some features might have to be dropped, others added, and still others changed. If you were hired to program to a specification, changes would have to be negotiated to ensure that you're not cheating your client out of something you assured them you could do. In this case, however, you are your own client, and so this spec document is just a gentle guide and a helpful map of what needs to get coded and what needs to be produced for the game.

In the next chapter, you'll learn about code libraries, data storage, and deck definition files, which are essential for a feature-rich video game.

Homework

Even high-tech video games can be reduced down to tabletop mechanics. Learning why games are fun to play is an important part of designing good games.

Try these analog hacks.

- Take a game that you like to play on the computer or console, and mentally deconstruct it. Determine what its game mechanics are. For instance, in Portal, the mechanic is solving intricate puzzles with fantasy portal physics. In Half Life, the mechanic is to shoot enemies while unraveling elements of a detailed story. In the Fallout series, the mechanic is storytelling and exploration.

Try to come up with a card game version of your favorite game. It doesn't have to be an exact match, but see how close you can get. Incorporate dice as needed.

CHAPTER 5

Database and Libraries

There are lots of ways to store data. In the Blackjack game, you stored the building blocks for a deck of playing cards in two tables—one for suits and one for values. That's a good method for small data sets that don't change from game to game, but it won't work if, for instance, it was possible for a player to level up and earn the ability to play with Jokers in the deck, because the tables defining the deck is hard-coded into the application.

To make permanent changes to a game environment, or to track player progress, scores, or preferences, you must create a data file outside of the .love file on your user's computer. Any game that keeps track of a player's progress has to do this, so it's a common task, but it does require additional Lua libraries designed to read and write data files.

The problem with pulling in more libraries than what Lua and LÖVE provide is that there's no reason to expect your users to coincidentally also have those libraries installed on their computer (and why would they, unless they were also Lua programmers?). There are two ways around this.

- Bundle the library with your game.

- Tell your users to install the libraries before trying to play your game.

© Seth Kenlon 2019
S. Kenlon, *Developing Games on the Raspberry Pi*,
https://doi.org/10.1007/978-1-4842-4170-7_5

The first option is most common in the game industry, but sometimes a library's license doesn't allow you to distribute it along with your own application. There's a strong culture of open source around Lua, so most Lua libraries are licensed to permit you to use them as you please as long as you credit their authors.

Some Lua libraries, however, depend on other applications running on a system, so they must be built especially for those systems. If you use advanced libraries, you have to maintain different builds—one for each platform. Usually, that means one build for Linux, one for Windows, and one for the Mac (unfortunately, Macs are hardware dependent, so you must have a recent Mac available, upon which you can build your release.)

Note   Some game developers choose not to bundle libraries to ensure that their users are free to manage which libraries are on their computer. While most users don't care about which obscure programming library is on their computers, they probably do care about getting security updates. A library "hidden away" in your `.love` file isn't updated along with the rest of a system. So when you do distribute a library, you owe it to your users to check in often with those libraries for important bug fixes and security updates, and then update your own application with the new versions.

Building libraries for each operating system you want your game to run on is an advanced topic outside the scope of this book. There are several good tools, such as win-builds.org, to help you, but this does require advanced knowledge of compiling software. For this reason, this book uses pure Lua libraries that can be bundled with your game and run on any platform with LÖVE installed.

Installing New Libraries

In most games, the kind of data needing storage is not very complex, so usually a simple configuration text file is sufficient. For Lua to know what to do with a text file, the text must have a predictable structure. Highly structured text storage forms a non-relational database that Lua loads into memory and uses just like any other variable you might create in Lua.

There are many popular formats for these kinds of files, including YAML, JSON, and INI. These formats allow you to store data in a consistent structure, which enables its parent application to accurately parse it.

One library (sometimes also called a *module*) that enables plain text configuration files is inifile. As its name suggests, it interacts with INI configuration files (if you don't know what that is, you'll write one soon, so don't worry).

The best place to find libraries for Lua is luarocks.org, a website dedicated to tracking and distributing Lua libraries. The site is useful for a new Lua programmer because it has several methods for you to search for libraries that you may not even know exist. As you become more familiar with programming, you'll get a feel for what to expect from any language. The luarocks command will prove far more efficient.

To install the luarocks command, either look for it in the dnfdragora application installer, or do the following in a terminal.

```
$ sudo dnf install luarocks
```

Once luarocks is installed, type it into a terminal to see a helpful message.

As the help message indicates, use the search argument to search for inifile, the library you need to parse text files in the INI format.

```
$ luarocks search inifile
Search results:
inifile
   1.0-2 (rockspec) - https://luarocks.org
   1.0-2 (src) - https://luarocks.org
   1.0-1 (rockspec) - https://luarocks.org
```

A common trap that programmers fall into is installing a library they need on *their* system, and then forgetting to bundle the library with their application. For that reason, you will not install inifile to your own system the way that you installed Lua or LÖVE. Instead, create a new folder in your home directory called config.

```
$ mkdir ~/config
```

Use luarocks to download and install the inifile package directly into your sample game folder.

```
$ cd ~/config
$ luarocks install --tree=local inifile
```

The --tree option tells luarocks to create a new folder, called local in this example, for all the files that would normally get installed. With this simple trick, you install all the dependency code you want to use in your project into the project directory itself. Your user doesn't have to worry about installing anything extra, because it's all contained in your project.

Now you know why you might want to add a library to a project and how to do it.

Now it's time to try some libraries to help with configuration files.

Configuration Files

To see how to interact with a text-based configuration file, open Geany and create a new file and enter the following sample data in INI format.

```
[player1]
name= slasher
defeated = zombie,vampire
level=7
[player2]
name= vecna
defeated = vampire,gug,shantak
level=8
```

Save the file as sample.ini into your home directory, *not* the config directory. After all, saving the configuration file into your LÖVE project directory is exactly what you're trying to avoid, because you want the configuration file to be separate from your application.

Imagine that this file is a save file for a game, with the progress of each player in each configuration block. Were this a real game, you would save a configuration file in a hidden folder named ~/., but for now, you can keep this sample unhidden.

Create a second file named main.lua and enter this simple program to parse the sample.ini file, change a value, and then update the config.

```
inifile = require('inifile')
-- find home directory
home = os.getenv('HOME')

-- detect path separator
-- returns '/' for Linux and Mac
-- and '\' for Windows
d = package.config:sub(1,1)
```

```
-- parse the INI file and
-- put values into a table called conf
conf = inifile.parse(home .. d .. 'sample.ini')

-- print the data for review
print(conf['player1']['name'])
print(conf['player1']['level'])
print(conf['player1']['defeated'])

-- level up player1
conf['player1']['level'] = tonumber(conf['player1']['level'])+1

-- save the change
inifile.save(home .. d .. 'sample.ini', conf)
```

This simple application detects the user's home directory, detects how the operating system finds its way to the home directory, parses the INI file, and then increments the level entry for player1 by 1.

Save the file. Change to the ~/config directory in a terminal, and then try running the application (it will fail, but that's intentional).

```
$ lua ./main.lua
lua: ./main.lua:4: module 'inifile' not found...
```

This tells you that Lua attempted to use the inifile library, but couldn't locate it because the library isn't installed on your system; it's installed in your project directory.

Setting the Package Path

When you created your own card dealer class for Blackjack, you used the require keyword to include your library with your main code. You must do the same for the inifile library.

Just as you generally know where you keep your files on your computer, Lua knows where libraries are normally kept on whatever system it's installed on. It keeps track of this information in a variable called package. path. If you tell Lua to require a package called foo, then Lua looks in all the locations listed in package.path. When it finds foo, it stops looking and proceeds to execute code. If foo is nowhere to be found, then it throws an error and the application crashes.

If you are adding a library to Lua (or a Lua-based application like LÖVE) that is outside the normal Lua package.path, then you must tell Lua where to look. If you don't, your program will crash because Lua can't find a library that you have told it to require.

You can see package.path yourself by launching Lua in a terminal.

```
$ Lua
> print(package.path)
./?.lua;/usr/share/lua/5.3/?.lua;/usr/share/lua/5.33/?/init.
lua;/usr/lib64/lua/5.3/?.lua;/usr/lib64/lua/5.3/?/init.lua
```

For a prettier view (and for a little practice with Lua), use the gmatch function of Lua to split each entry, separated by semicolons.

```
> for s in package.path:gmatch("([^;]+)") do print(s) end
./?.lua
/usr/share/lua/5.3/?.lua
/usr/share/lua/5.3/?/init.lua
/usr/lib64/lua/5.3/?.lua
```

When require is used in these examples, Lua first searches the current directory for anything ending in .lua. If nothing applicable is found, Lua knows to search /usr/share/lua/5.3 and then /usr/share/lua/5.3/? (Lua itself substitutes ? with *the name of the library you provide in* require *statements*).

You can append entries to package.path in your program so that if you add a new library outside of Lua or LÖVE, Lua knows where to find it. To do that, you must know where to find the libraries yourself.

You told Luarocks to install inifile to local, so you know where to start. There are two easy ways to find the actual code of the library you installed: the ls command and the find command.

If you're not entirely sure what you're looking for, you can use the ls --recursive command to list all directories and all the directories in those directories (and so on).

```
$ ls --recursive ./local
local/:
lib/   share/
local/lib:
luarocks/
local/lib/luarocks:
rocks/
local/lib/luarocks/rocks:
inifile/   manifest
local/lib/luarocks/rocks/inifile:
1.0-2/
local/lib/luarocks/rocks/inifile/1.0-2:
inifile-1.0-2.rockspec   rock_manifest
local/share:
lua/
local/share/lua:
5.3/
local/share/lua/5.3:
inifile.lua
```

At the very bottom of the list is the inifile.lua file, which is—as its file extension .lua suggests—the Lua library that you seek.

Note   There is a related package path called `package.cpath` that locates complex libraries written in the C programming language. These libraries use the file extension `.so` on Linux, `.dll` on Windows, and `.dylib` on Macs.

If you had already known you were looking for a `.lua` file, then you could also have used the `find` command.

```
$ find ./local -name "*.lua"
./local/share/lua/5.3/inifile.lua
```

The end results of the commands are the same: you get the path to the library or libraries you need to add to the very top of your `main.lua` code.

```
package.path = package.path .. ';local/share/lua/5.3/?.lua'
```

This simple statement sets `package.path` to be *whatever it already is,* and then appends (..) the `local` directory. It also replaces any instance of ? with *whatever is required.*

Note   If you read other people's Lua code, you might see the alternate method of pointing Lua to a library. Sometimes, a programmer provides the path to the library manually in the `require` statement, using dots as delimiters: `require('lib.inifile.inifile')`. This isn't wrong or bad, but it is very specific to a *single* library file. Not all libraries consist of just one file, so that method is less flexible than providing the `package.path`.

Try your program again. This time, it is successful.

```
$ lua ./main.lua
slasher
7
zombie,vampire
```

The file was parsed correctly. Now check the original sample.ini file to see if player1's level was updated. To see the contents of a file quickly in a terminal, you can use the cat command, which is short for *concatenate* (so you are, in effect, concatenating the file to nothing, so its contents are just printed to your terminal).

```
$ cat ~/sample.ini
[player1]
name= slasher
defeated = zombie,vampire
level=8

[player2]
name= vecna
defeated = vampire,gug,shantak
level=8
```

Lua has parsed, read, and written a plain text configuration using a local library.

Deck Building

Having completed the exercise in this chapter, you not only know how to store data on your user's computer, but you also know how to define data structures in a file to have it imported by your application. That means you

CHAPTER 5   DATABASE AND LIBRARIES

don't have to define a deck of complex battle cards in the main code of
your application, which means a smaller file for your executable code and
a lot less clutter in your main script.

For the Blackjack game, the card deck was a simple 52-card poker
deck. Your current project, Battlejack, can use a standard card deck, but
part of the fun of programming digitally is that you can generate game
assets without the costly manufacturing bills involved in creating a new
deck of cards in the physical world. It doesn't make sense to limit the game
to a standard poker deck when you can invent any theme you want for
your game.

Regardless of your artistic skill or access to artwork, 52 cards is a lot of
cards to make. It's not impossible (there are more than 10,000 Magic: The
Gathering cards, and 2,000 in Magic Online), but for an independent game
developer, it's a tall order. When determining the assets for a game, it's
important to look critically at what is necessary and what is just nice to have.

For this project, even though the design assets were 52 cards, there
were actually only 10 unique values: 1 through 10. For every iteration of
cards 1 to 10, there were three cards worth 10 (Jack, King, and Queen).
Furthermore, although the dev deck had four suits, the suits actually had
no effect on the game, so those can be thrown out.

To create player identities, the alpha version of the game used red and
black, and since that's easy and classic, the digital version can keep that.
For accessibility, the digital version will also use a symbol along with the
opposing colors, since not everyone can see the color red.

To make the game a little more exciting, the digital version of Battlejack
will enable players to "level up" as they continue to play. Levels in any
game are a mix of rewards and, essentially, penalties; the players level up
and become more powerful, but only to face new challenges. That means
the digital deck will have a small subset of extra cards that are shuffled into
the game, throwing off the predictability of how often certain values are
drawn, and a second subset of cards that serve as "power ups" granting the
player a free bonus (anywhere from a +1 to +3) to their hand.

There isn't much to this dataset, but it should be expressed separately from the user data because it is not data that is meant to change. It defines the virtual deck of cards, and that's all. Tracking which cards have been drawn during a game must be done by the application itself, because it gets reset every time a new game is started. Any permanent rewards, penalties, or level data is written to the user data file.

Take a moment to think about what kind of deck you want to use for your Battlejack implementation, or download and use the deck provided with this book. (The art is licensed under a Creative Commons license, so you may use the artwork for any purpose). Once you have decided on a theme, create a project folder called battlejack. Create font and img directories within your project folder, as usual.

Create a deck definition file called deck.ini and save it into your project directory. You can customize the definition file to suit your custom theme, or if you are using the art available with this book, you can use the following.

```
[red]
mystic = 1
bard = 2
arcanist = 3
archer = 4
goblin = 5
construct = 6
cavalry = 7
priest = 8
fighter = 9
wizard = 10
cavalry = 10
knight  = 10
```

```
[black]
mystic = 1
bard = 2
arcanist = 3
archer = 4
goblin = 5
construct = 6
cavalry = 7
priest = 8
fighter = 9
wizard = 10
cavalry = 10
knight  = 10

[earn]
zealot  = 6
cultist = 7
charm   = 8
orc     = 9
god     = 10

[up]
sun     = 1
bird    = 1
sword   = 1
ram     = 2
skull   = 2
templar = 2
weep    = 3
plague  = 3
```

That's just 25 cards to generate; although in a pinch it can be done with just three (one for all face cards, one for all earned cards, and one for all powerup cards). That's manageable, so now all that's left to do is make them. And that's just what you'll do in the next chapter.

Homework

Installing and learning new libraries is an important part of programming. Nobody codes everything from scratch unless absolutely necessary, because there are so many great libraries out there with much of your work already done for you.

Try the following hacks.

- INI files store key and value pairs; one word correlates to exactly one other word or number. For more complex data structures, there is a format called YAML, which allows you to define multiple levels of information for everything in your data set.

Install `lua-yaml` or a similar library for parsing YAML and try to parse some sample data.

For an example of a working script, download the code files for this chapter from this book's code repository.

CHAPTER 6

Graphics

Everyone knows graphics are important for games, but gamers acknowledge that there's something even more important than graphics: the game. A good game is a game that's challenging and fun. Graphics, while important, don't make a game.

But most modern players expect graphics in their games, and given that you're programming for a graphical game engine, you do need graphics. And if you're going to have graphics in your game, you want them to look as good as possible.

If you're not a natural illustrator and don't have access to one, making your graphics look good seems like a tall order. And if you're not familiar with graphic applications on Linux, it seems impossible. This chapter teaches you the basics of a few of the best Linux graphics applications and provides you with some tips and tricks to make great graphics, even if you think you have no artistic skills.

Design by Genre

The word *genre* is an art term meaning a category or style. It's a term meant to be broad and nonspecific. If you're fortunate enough to be able to hire an artist to do artwork for your game, then a genre is useful to convey to the artist what they should be aiming for. When it's entirely up to you to design the game's graphics, a genre gives you a target to aim for when gathering and creating all the different artistic elements that you need.

© Seth Kenlon 2019
S. Kenlon, *Developing Games on the Raspberry Pi*,
https://doi.org/10.1007/978-1-4842-4170-7_6

When the same person programming a game also has to design the game's look and feel, one of the greatest concerns is investment of time and effort. After all, you can't afford to just spend your time on art when there's still code to be written. To help you stay on track, keep in mind three basic tenants to successful graphics.

- *Genre*. Limit yourself to elements within your declared genre.

- *Consistency*. Design once, and then duplicate. If you do anything consistently enough, it becomes your *style*.

- *Minimalism*. Convey only the most vital information and let your players read between the lines. The less you do, the less you can mess up.

Before you sit down to create your game art, stop and think of a genre to serve as your central design theme. Your theme can be anything, just think about what appeals to you or to your intended audience. Think in terms of a broad genre. The more general your initial concept, the easier it is to hit your mark in the end. Much of the frustration that non-artists experience when they attempt to make art is because they see clearly in their mind what they want, but lack the artistic skills to make it happen. Protect yourself by avoiding specifics.

Here are some examples of some broad themes.

- Retro 8-bit video games

- Victorian England

- Horror

- Mysteries of the ancient world

- Saturday morning cartoons

- Anime or manga

- Comic book

- Fantasy

- Urban

- Cyberpunk

It can also be fun to mash up two different genres. Instead of settling for just a fantasy game, why not make rock-a-billy fantasy? Or cyberpunk in the Old West? Or a cartoon horror game? Mix it up. Force yourself to invent a rationale for an unlikely combination, and see what happens.

Let the Fonts Do the Talking

Once you have thought of a genre (or two) for your game, go on a font hunt. Fonts are a great way to convey a theme quickly, and since there are so many open source fonts out there, it's one of the lowest investments of effort on your part (see Figure 6-1). There's a font out there for every genre, so go find one and bring it into your project to kick-start your thematic vision.

Note   Fonts are just like everything else you find online or on most computers. They're *licensed* for use, meaning that if you find a font you like on a Windows or Mac computer, it's only licensed for you to use on that one computer. You're not allowed to redistribute it with your game. So when looking for fonts, make sure its license permits it to be redistributed.

Some of the best open or redistributable font websites include

- FontLibrary.org

- slackermedia.info/sprints

- FontSquirrel.com

- TheLeagueofMoveableType.com

- DaFont.com (use the site's filters to view only free and open source fonts)

If you choose a highly stylized font, then you might need two fonts: one for big titles consisting of only a few words at a time, and one simpler font that's easier to read for text that users need to read often or quickly.

Figure 6-1. *Fonts are worth 1000 words*

The important thing is that the font or fonts you choose speak to your theme. It's alright if your fonts are a little cliché as long as they enforce your genre. If you're not sure of what type of font to use, go look at some movie posters or book covers to get an idea of how fonts are used to convey the genre of the story being told.

Before continuing, download a font or two to your Downloads folder. This example uses the Arkham font from DaFont.com (www.dafont.com/arkham.font), a free font with no restrictions on redistribution.

To install a font, do the following.

1. Open a file manager window and navigate to your Downloads directory. Most font downloads are zipped, so you must unarchive them to install them.

2. If you prefer to work with GUI tools, install xarchiver in dnfdragora.

3. If you prefer to work in a terminal, install p7zip-full with apt.

   ```
   $ sudo dnf install p7zip-full
   ```

4. Next, create a local font folder located at ~/.local/share/fonts.

   ```
   $ mkdir -p ~/.local/share/fonts
   ```

5. To do this in the GUI, open a file manager by double-clicking the Home icon on your desktop. Right-click in any blank space in the file manager window. Select Options ➤ Show Hidden Files, and then navigate to .local/share. In the share directory, right-click any blank area and select New ➤ Directory. Name the new directory fonts.

6. Create a subdirectory in ~/.local/share/fonts for the first letter of each font you are installing, and then copy the TTF or OTF files to the appropriate place.

7. To copy the files, you must unarchive your font downloads. Most font archives can be unarchived with p7zip, but you can also use other unarchiver tools as needed.

```
$ cd Downloads
$ 7z x arkhamfonts.zip
$ tar xvf nouveau.tar.bz2
```

8. Once unarchived, you can copy the files to their destination.

```
$ mkdir -p ~/.local/share/fonts/a
$ cp ~/Downloads/arkhamfonts/ark*ttf ~/.local/
share/fonts/a
```

In the GUI, right-click a font archive and select Open with ➤ xarchiver. Drag and drop font files from the xarchiver window to the directory matching the first letter of the font name.

Color Scheme

The last thematic element you must decide upon is a color scheme. While some genres have specific colors associated with them, there's a lot of freedom in this aspect of design. While the Old West is often associated with browns and yellows, and a technical future world often is painted in black and neon green, you can use your own color palette in any genre as long as your colors are consistent and somehow relate to one another in a pleasing way.

The problem for non-artists is finding colors that match.

To solve this problem, all you have to do is generate a color palette from an existing image. Search the Internet or your own hard drive for an image that you like. It doesn't have to be a free-licensed photo and it doesn't have to match the genre for your game, because the image is only going to be used to generate colors. Just pick an image that you enjoy looking at.

To generate a color scheme from a photograph, do the following.

1. Install Image Magick.

   ```
   $ sudo dnf install imagemagick
   ```

2. Download the image to your Pi.

3. Run the following Image Magick command, adjusting ~/path/to/image.png to match whatever photo you have downloaded.

   ```
   $ convert ~/path/to/image.png -geometry 16x16
   -colors 8 \
   -unique-colors -scale 4000% ~/scheme.png
   ```

4. Take a look at the resulting color scheme.

   ```
   $ display ~/scheme.png
   ```

The colors you get back as scheme.png are more or less an average of dominant colors (it's not mathematically sound, but it's a rough approximation). Use these colors to guide your design (see Figure 6-2).

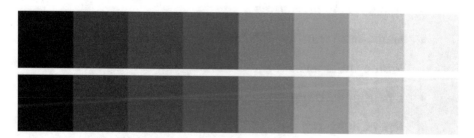

Figure 6-2. Color scheme

Graphics

When it comes to the actual graphics for a game, there are three areas of interest you must consider: the background, the foreground, and widgets.

Widgets and menu screens are where the theme is most obvious, because everything is largely static. You can use a thematic background and some genre-appropriate buttons, and the stage is set.

The background of each level is a good place to set mood and tone. It usually needs to be minimal so that it doesn't take attention away from the elements that the player is interacting with, but it's a good opportunity for you to convey elements of your theme. For instance, if your game is set in Victorian England, then decorating the corners of the background with a damask print or a regal design can help convey the setting. It's also a good opportunity to use some of the colors of your primary scheme, which can also help set the mood: a bright and cheerful background sends a different message than a dark one.

The foreground consists of all the elements your player cares about, such as their player character, their enemies, loot, tutorial messages, and so on. These elements can also be themed to match your color scheme and game theme.

Finding graphics can be difficult, but there are online repositories of free game art, including

- Itch.io/game-assets/free

- GameArt2d.com/freebies.html

- Kenney.nl/assets

- OpenGameArt.org

- OpenClipArt.org

There's a lot of flexibility in the foreground elements. As long as the game *world* matches your genre, you can drop characters—good or evil—into it, and gamers won't think twice about it. After all, one of the most famous games of all time is ostensibly about the exciting world of plumbing, and yet the main enemies are sentient toadstools and turtles.

Even though you may gather game assets from the Creative Commons, you're still probably going to find that you have to adapt or modify them. The Raspberry Pi comes fully equipped for game development, graphic design included.

Card Design with GIMP

GIMP (GNU Image Manipulation Program) is an all-purpose graphics creation application. You can use it to modify photographs, textures, and existing graphics, and combine them all together to provide you with your game assets, or you can create graphics from nothing but your own ideas.

The barrier to getting started with GIMP isn't artistic skill so much as comprehending and learning the many tools that GIMP has to offer. Entire books have been written about it, there are tutorial websites dedicated to it, and it has thorough documentation, so this section steps you through the process of using the tools that apply to the current goal: creating playing cards for Battlejack. Stepping through this won't teach you everything about GIMP, but it demonstrates the general process and some of the common tools.

Install

There are a few different ways to install GIMP. The easiest way gets you an old version of GIMP, and while there's nothing wrong with that under normal circumstances, you're a software developer now so there's no reason to settle for second best. Instead of installing using the Synaptic application installer or the dnf command in a terminal, you can install the latest version, as described at www.gimp.org/downloads/.

The latest build of GIMP is delivered using Flatpak, a software installer method similar in spirit to dnf. To use Flatpak, it must be installed.

```
$ sudo dnf install flatpak
```

Once Flatpak has been installed, use it to install GIMP.

```
$ sudo flatpak install \
https://flathub.org/repo/appstream/org.gimp.GIMP.flatpakref
```

Once GIMP and all of its dependencies have been installed, you must log out of the Enlightenment desktop, and then log back in so that it recognizes updates from Flatpak. If you don't want to do that just now, you can launch GIMP manually, as described in the gimp.org download instructions.

```
$ flatpak run org.gimp.GIMP//stable
```

In the future (after a reboot), you can find GIMP in your application menu.

The GIMP interface consists of three main regions: the toolbox is full of all the tools that you use to compose graphics, the main window contains any graphics that you are working on, and the contextual docks provide extra options based on what you're doing.

In the first part of this chapter, you defined a theme or a combination of themes, and collected suitable assets, such as fonts and clip art. GIMP allows you to composite them together.

New Document

To create a new document in GIMP, do the following.

1. In the GIMP window, click File ➤ New.

2. In the Create a New Image dialog box that appears, set the unit of measure to mm. Set the image width to 63.5mm and the height to 88.9mm. These measurements are those of a standard US poker playing card.

3. Since screen size and printed size are different, click the Advanced Options link at the bottom of the window and set the resolution of your image to 100 DPI. Any lower, and your image may look too small or pixelated on standard displays. Any higher, and your image will be too large to fit on the screen.

Note   For serious design work, it's not uncommon to design at a higher resolution, just in case you want to also print the designs you create for onscreen display or to account for the eventual increase in graphic resolution. For instance, as of this writing, it's common for gamers to own 100 DPI monitors sized 1920×1080, but in a few years, 4K monitors and greater will be the default. If you design in higher resolutions, you safeguard against increasing resolution, but if you do that during this chapter, you have to scale the image down in LÖVE.

Color Scheme

So that you have it handy, open the scheme.png color scheme file you created earlier. If you didn't create a color scheme file, that's alright, just keep your color scheme in mind.

Color selection in a graphics application is a lot like variables in programming. It's something you end up doing a lot more often than you think you should have to, although GIMP makes it easy. GIMP is smart enough to map a color scheme to a *palette*.

1. To see your GIMP palettes, go to the Window menu
    ➤ Dockable Dialogs ➤ Palettes. This embeds a new
    panel displaying color palettes, including one called
    Colormap of Image, which is your color scheme
    imported as a palette (Figure 6-3).

Figure 6-3. *Creating a colormap in GIMP*

2. Right-click your palette and select Duplicate Palette
    to create an editable copy.

3. Double-click the duplicate and give it a name,
    such as cardscheme. A named palette becomes
    permanent.

4. You may now close the color scheme file so that only
    your blank card appears in your workspace.

5. Your named color scheme remains. Right-click it
    and select Edit Palette to open the Palette Editor tab.
    This displays your color scheme so that you can use
    it as a reference when choosing the colors in your
    design.

6. GIMP uses a tabbed interface to manage open
    files, so to get back to your card design, click the
    appropriate tab at the top of the window.

Text Elements

Eventually, you must create cards for each card listed in the deck.ini file,
but this example creates a wizard card with a value of 10 to ensure that the
initial design accounts for a long title and a double-digit value.

1. Select the Text tool from the Tool Options panel, or
    press T on your keyboard.

2. Click near the top-left corner of your card, but don't start typing anything yet. When you click, a contextual tool-based panel appears below your toolbox. Since the text tool is active, you see options for text. Pick a font within your theme, and set the size to 60 or so.

3. To set the color of your text, click the box labelled Color. A color picker window appears. Its default view is the GIMP color picker, but there are tabs along the top of window Figure 6-4.

Figure 6-4. *Viewing a color scheme in GIMP*

4. Click the right-most tab to view your custom palette and choose a color for your text.

5. Click the OK button.

6. Now that you have your tool configured, type the title of the card: **Wizard**. Don' worry if you positioned your text too far to the right such that the whole word won't fit; you can fix that later.

7. Press the Esc key to exit text mode.

Time to Save

It's never too early to start saving your work. To save your document, go to the File menu and select Save. You can save the document anywhere you please, but it's best to keep project work together, so saving it into your battlejack directory is best.

However, GIMP files are a special .xcf format intended as an uncompressed master copy, not as a file for everyday use, so in the end you'll export to .png or .jpg. Intermediate files that are necessary to create assets but that do not ship with a game are generically called *source* files. It's not uncommon to place them in a directory all their own, and then exclude that directory from your final .love package.

1. Using the GIMP save dialog, create a new directory, called src, in your battlejack project.

2. In src, create another directory called img, and save your file into it with the name red-10-wizard.xcf.

Moving Layers

When you typed text onto your card, you created a new layer. If you don't see a Layers docker in your GIMP window, go to the Window ➤ Dockable Dialogs menu and select Layers to open it or bring it to the top of a docking panel.

Layers are like sheets of cellophane placed on top of a canvas. They're transparent until you "paint" something on them, and even then you can always move or remove the layer entirely because you haven't painted on your canvas, but on a transparent layer above it.

As long as the text layer is selected (and it is, by default, because it was the most recent one you created), its bounding box is a yellow and black dotted-line. By default, a layer uses up only as much space as it needs, but if you need to make a layer bigger, go to the Layer menu and select Layer to Image Size.

1. To move a layer, select the Move tool in the Tool Options panel, or press M. As always, the Tool Options panel displays configuration choices for that tool. Select the "Move the active layer" option.

2. Click your card and drag your mouse to move the active layer. Position your text where you think the title of each card looks best.

Backdrops

To help the player focus on what's important, it often helps to add backdrops. A backdrop separates important information, especially text, from the background image.

1. To add a layer between the background and a foreground layer, right-click the background layer and select New Layer.

2. In the New Layer window, name the layer backdrop and set the "Fill with" field to Transparency so that the layer is filled with a transparent alpha channel.

3. Select the Rectangle Select tool from the Tool Options panel, or press R on your keyboard. Using this selection tool, select an area around the title. It might be hard to tell, but you're not selecting the title text or the white background behind it. You're selecting a portion of the invisible layer between them.

4. Click the top color swatch under the toolbox. In the color picker that appears, select the Palette tab and select a color within your color scheme.

5. Click the Edit menu at the top of the GIMP window, and select Fill with FG Color (FG stands for *foreground*).

6. To exit selection mode, press the Esc key on your keyboard.

Color Code and Value

The card still needs a value. According to deck.ini, its value is 10. Repeat the previous process to create a value indicator.

Since Battlejack's opposing sides are differentiated by color (red against black), use red as the backdrop color. If you don't have red in your color scheme, you must adapt. You can still use your color scheme as a guide, though. RGB colors are defined by three numbers ranging from 0 to 255: the first number is for red, the second for green, and the third for blue. These values are visible in the right column of the GIMP color picker window. Look at a color in your palette and shift its numbers such that the highest number is in the color you want to create within the same scheme.

For instance, assume you have a green defined in your palette with these values: Red 11, Green 14, Blue 8. To produce a red similar in "feel", shift each number one position to the left so that the number in the Blue slot now goes to Green, the number in the Green slot goes to Red, and the number in Red wraps around to Blue: Red 14, Green 8, Blue 11.

The resulting red shade may not be exactly what you want, but this trick produces something in the same mood as the rest of your color scheme, and you can adjust it manually with one of the color wheels in the color picker tabs.

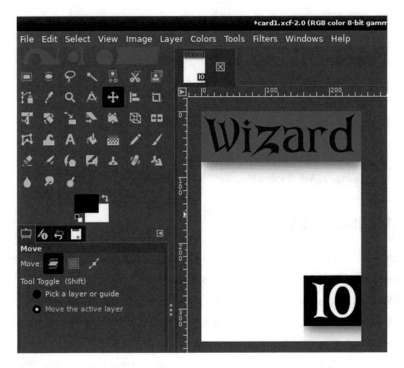

Figure 6-5. *Card design*

Background Image

The card design is basically finished. It has the requisite information on it, so all it needs now is an image. Find an image that you feel might represent a wizard. Think abstractly. It's easier to find an image that suggests wizardry than to find a free image of exactly what you see in your mind's eye when you think of a wizard.

For example, you might be able to find a series of icons for fantasy roles consisting of wands, swords, battle axes, and so on. Even if you only find five or six icons, you could reuse those depending on the broad category of each card (a wand for each magic user, a sword for generic fighters, an axe for particularly powerful fighters, and so on.

116

Alternatively, you can borrow from Magic: the Gathering, which bases all player abilities on five different types of land. Backgrounds for video games or even landscape photography are easy to find. Add some "flavor text" on the card to explain how the land depicted has influenced the wizard that the card represents.

The possibilities are endless, so use your imagination. If you can't find suitable images for this project, you can use images provided along with the source code for this book. The images are from the tabletop game Petition, designed by the author, and illustrated by Nikolai Mamashev in Krita on Linux. All assets are provided under the Creative Commons Attribution-ShareAlike license.

1. To bring in an image, click the layer named Background. This layer is the base layer of your GIMP document.

2. Click the File menu and select Open as layers.

3. The image you choose from the file chooser is imported into your document above the Background layer but below your backdrops and text. The image may be too large, but you can fix that with the Scale tool.

4. As needed, select the Scale tool from the toolbox, or press Shift+S on your keyboard.

5. Click the image that you want to resize and use the selection bounding box or the dialog box to scale the image to better fit into your card design.

6. Press the Return key or click the Scale button to accept the change.

Other tools you can use to fit an image into your design include the Rotate and Flip tools. Try them out and see what looks best.

Integration

To bring elements of the card design together, and as an excuse to learn more GIMP tricks, the final step is to make the card look more like an intentional design and less like something cobbled together from disparate sources. You can try one or none of these techniques, depending on what you like in card design.

The first technique is to add a subtle drop shadow to the backdrop to suggest that the "meta" game information is not part of the wizard. In other words, you're acknowledging that in real life, people don't walk around with banners and titles and a number value assigned to them.

1. To add a drop shadow, select a backdrop layer and then click Filters ➤ Light and Shadow.

2. There are currently two different drop shadow filters: one is permanent and the other ("legacy") creates a new layer just for the drop shadow. Use either one, but remember: less is more. A subtle shadow says more than a big, bold shadow that draws attention to itself.

3. Another integration technique is to merge the meta information of the card with the "flavor" (graphic). You can do that by blending text into the image. First, right-click the 10 layer in the Layers docker and select Text to Path.

4. Locate the Paths docker by clicking the Windows menu and selecting Dockable Dialogs ➤ Paths.

5. In the Paths palette, there is now an outline of the text element 10. The outline is a vector path— a mathematical formula that GIMP doesn't see as a graphic but as a guide for graphical manipulation. Right-click the path and select Path to Selection. The text on the card is now selected.

6. Navigate back to the Layers docker. Click the eye icon to the left of the 10 layer to hide the text, and then select the red backdrop layer.

7. With the shape of the 10 still selected, press the Delete key on your keyboard, or go to the Edit menu and select Clear. This erases red from your backdrop in the shape of the number 10. You can see right through the backdrop to the image beneath.

8. To remove the active selection, go to Select and choose None, or press Shift+Ctrl+A on your keyboard.

There's a lot more you can do in GIMP, so try out some subtle effects, brushes, and composite modes. Work in layers, so that anything you do can't be undone later if necessary. GIMP is a powerful tool, so investing in a good tutorial book or spending time on some tutorial sites is effort well spent.

Of course, you don't have to use this example as a blueprint for your design. Come up with your own ideas, tap into what appeals to you, and create it Figure 6-6.

Figure 6-6. *Art by Shiroikuro, Dogchicken, and Solkap*

Exporting from GIMP

The native format of GIMP files is a multilayered and uncompressed
.xcf file. It's intended as a project file for use within GIMP. It wouldn't
make sense to use it anywhere else, especially not in a LÖVE game. After
completing each card, you must export it to a common graphic format like
PNG or JPEG.

To export an image from GIMP, go to the File menu and select
Export as.

In the file chooser that appears, navigate to your battlejack project
directory, name the file in a standard format, such as red-10-wizard.png,
and then export the image to the img directory.

Homework

Getting to know GIMP is important if you plan on doing graphics work,
whether you anticipate creating promotional web banners or all the
graphics in your game. Spend some time getting to understand how GIMP

works, and enjoy the freedom of doing complex graphical work without having to pay a "rental" fee each month the way that designers tied down to big-name competitors do.

There are several other excellent graphic applications on Linux. GIMP is good at collage (professionally known as *compositing*), and can be used for digital painting if you download a good set of brushes.

The following are some other graphic applications.

- Inkscape is a vector drawing application, good for precision illustration, layout, and graphics that scale infinitely.

- mtPaint is a bitmap drawing application good for pixel art. It's a small application that runs very well on the Raspberry Pi.

- Krita is a digital painting application. It's a big application and doesn't run well on the current Raspberry Pi.

- MyPaint is a digital painting application for small drawings; it runs on the latest Pi.

CHAPTER 7

Menu Design

With all of your designs and assets ready, it's finally time to start coding Battlejack. When you sit down to write code, it's essential to have the design specs on hand. Here's a review of how Battlejack works.

When the game launches, the player is greeted with a menu screen that allows the user to start a new game, resume a saved game, adjust settings for full-screen or windowed display, or return to a game already in session.

During game play, the user clicks their own deck to draw a card. During their turn, the player clicks and drags cards to either the dealer's stash to cancel out a card in play, or to their own score box to add their card to their own stash. Onscreen prompts alert the player of their choices Figure 7-1.

If a player attempts to cancel a dealer card out with a less powerful card (trying to cancel a five-strength card with a three-strength card, for example), nothing happens. The player may add powerups or additional cards to complete the action, or click and drag the card back into their hand to continue.

© Seth Kenlon 2019
S. Kenlon, *Developing Games on the Raspberry Pi*,
https://doi.org/10.1007/978-1-4842-4170-7_7

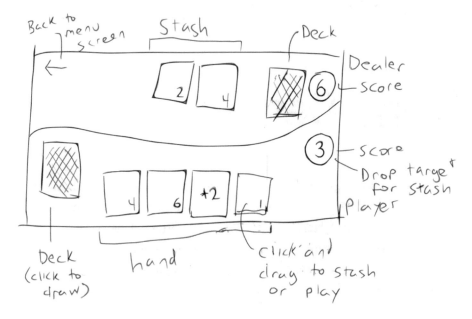

Figure 7-1. *Rough draft for the game UI*

The first task for this chapter is to build a basic menu screen that successfully proceeds to an empty game screen, with an option to return to the menu screen so a player can save or quit.

Main Framework

Launch Geany and navigate to your battlejack project directory.

Create three new files: main.lua, menu.lua, and game.lua. Since LÖVE always launches a file called main.lua, you must use that as a kind of control center for the different parts of your game. The main.lua file serves as the engine keeping the game open; it invokes the menu and game states.

The menu.lua and game.lua files are the game states, so you must require them in the main file. In the main.lua file, enter the usual setup code.

```
require("menu")
require("game")

WIDE, HIGH = 960,720

love.window.setTitle(' Battlejack ')
love.window.setMode( WIDE, HIGH )

function love.load()
end

function love.draw()
end
```

Your application can only be in one state at a time. A player cannot be in the menu while playing the game. So whenever a game state is activated, it creates a token to designate that it is the current active state.

The token can be called anything, but for clarity, call it STATE and set it, initially, to nothing. Place it near the top of the main.lua file.

```
WIDE, HIGH = 960,720
STATE      = nil
```

The main loop's job is relatively simple: draw on screen whatever happens to be the active STATE.

```
function love.draw()
    STATE.draw()
end
```

The first thing that you want your player to see is the menu, so for the first action upon launch, make a call to your (currently empty) menu code. Since your menu is devoid of code, invent a function name to designate the act of switching to the menu; the term activate seems logical, so use that.

```
function love.load()
    menu.activate()
end
```

Your game won't launch yet, because you're referencing two empty files, and you call functions that don't yet exist and use variables that never get set. You fix that in the next section.

Switching Modes

A menu screen needs, at the very least, a few menu selections. It also needs to set the STATE token so that the main loop knows the current game state.

In previous exercises, you have treated all variables equally, but in fact, there are broadly two different kinds of variables: local variables and global variables. A *local variable* only needs to be used within one Lua file (in other languages, a *class*), but a *global variable* can be used across files.

In context of this project, the STATE variable must be a global variable because it is set by either the menu or game, and then is sent back to main for use. Something local to only the menu can be a local variable because no other file in this project ever draws a menu.

Pragmatically, all variables can be global; however, it's better to differentiate when possible so that your application can manage its memory more effectively.

Start your menu.lua file with the following code.

```
menu = {}

local entries = { "New game", "Load saved",
        "Window mode", "Save", "Quit" }

function menu.activate()
    STATE = menu
end
```

This code includes a few vital elements: it sets the STATE global variable so that main.lua knows the game state, and it creates the .activate function as a gateway into the menu from the main loop. It also sets up the menu entries.

To print the menu entries on the screen, use a .draw function specific to the menu file. Your main.lua file call this function as long as menu is the active state, because in love.draw() you call STATE.draw().

```
function menu.draw()
    love.graphics.setBackgroundColor(0.1,0.1,0.1)
    for i=1,5 do
    -- menu text                        x    y
    love.graphics.print(entries[i], 45, 10+i*16)
    end
end
```

In this code, you use a for loop to cycle through the number of entries in the menu. For each iteration of the loop, LÖVE prints the corresponding menu entry as defined at the top of the file.

Since the menu is the first and only thing invoked by main.lua, you can now launch your application now to see what you have so far.

The first problem you are likely to notice is that there's no way to select any of the menu entries. One of the many benefits of LÖVE is its keypressed function, which is perfect for game and menu navigation (this is discussed in the next section).

First, you may as well put in some basic code for the game screen, so that once the menu is operational, you can tell the difference between the menu screen and the game world.

The bare minimum is sufficient.

```
game = {}

function game.activate()
    STATE = game
end
```

```
function game.draw()
    love.graphics.setBackgroundColor(0.2,0.3,0.5)
end
```

You can't get there yet, but at least it exists, and with a background color set, you'll know it when you see it.

Menu Selection

There are two aspects of menu selection: the code that drives the actual selection and the onscreen representation of that selection so that the player knows what's selected. Both need a designator, so create a variable to keep track which menu entry is the current selection.

```
function menu.activate()
    STATE = menu
    selection = 1
end
```

For the player, a visual cue is useful. There are several ways to implement a selection marker for a text menu, but for now, just draw a simple character next to the active entry by checking the value of the selection variable. Of course, at this point, the selection variable can only be 1 because nothing has changed yet in your code; but that won't be true for much longer.

Update your menu.draw() function so it matches this:

```
function menu.draw()
    love.graphics.setBackgroundColor(0.1,0.1,0.1)

    for i=1,5 do
    if i == selection then
            love.graphics.print(">", 30, 10+i*16)
    end
```

```
    -- menu text
    love.graphics.print(entries[i], 45, 10+i*16)
    end
end
```

You can launch the game to see the > marker on the first selection.

When a user presses a key on the keyboard, the computer receives a keycode signal. This is known as an input *event*. Depending on your language and keyboard layout, your operating system translates keycodes to specific letters, numbers, or characters. That's built into any operating system, and it's why you can interact with your computer.

The only reason a specific application reacts to a number or character or symbol, however, is because it is programmed to do something when a keypress event is received. LÖVE features the keypressed( ) function, which listens for keypress events and lets you define what should happen with each keypress event.

For menu navigation, you must define what the menu must do when it receives an Up arrow or a Down arrow event. These events both toggle the active selection, which is currently set to 1 by default. Since the selection variable is set to 1 when the application starts, the active selection is the first in the list. To make the active selection second on the list, the selection variable must be incremented when the Down arrow is pressed, and decremented when the Up arrow is pressed. If you're good with math, you might detect an exception to this rule already; if not, you'll discover it soon.

In addition to moving the selection designator around, the menu should respond when the Return key is pressed.

A keypress event sends LÖVE three pieces of information: the key that was pressed, the scancode of the key (layout-independent code of a key), and whether or not the key was pressed once or pressed repeatedly (the definition of a *repeat* depends on the user's system settings). For this menu screen, all you need to process is which key has been pressed. Detecting the key and taking action upon it is achieved with an if loop.

```
function menu.keypressed(k)
    if k == "down" then
    selection = selection+1
    elseif k == "up" then
    selection = selection-1
    elseif k == "return" or k == " " then
    if selection == 1 then
            game.new()
    elseif selection == 2 then
            game.load()
        elseif selection == 3 then
        window.activate()
    elseif selection == 4 then
            save()
    elseif selection == 5 then
        love.event.quit()
    end
    elseif k == "escape" then
        game.activate()
    end
end
```

It's a common convention in games to use the Esc key to call and dismiss a menu screen, so pressing the Esc key goes back to the game screen.

To differentiate when a user is starting a new game and resuming a saved game, the preceding code sample invents some nonexistent functions, such as game.new() and game.load(). It's alright that these don't work yet, because you'll create them later.

If you test the application, you will probably notice that the application crashes if you try to move up from the top selection or down from the bottom selection. If you're not new to programming, you probably predicted this issue, but if you're new to all of this, then it's useful to witness the crash and then to follow the logic and math that causes it.

The selection starts out as 1. Pressing the Down arrow increments selection to 2, then 3, 4, and 5. All of these numbers correspond to the existing five menu entries. If selection gets incremented once more to 6, however, LÖVE doesn't know what to do because there is no sixth menu entry next to which it can draw the > selection symbol.

To solve this bug, you must catch when selection would normally become either 0 or 6 and impose an existing number. A user would expect a menu selection to *wrap*: when you scroll past the bottom of a list, the active selection becomes the top of the list.

First, define in one place the number of menu entries there are by adding the following line near the top of your code and near your other local variable.

```
local menmax = 5
```

To do the math to fix a selection that goes out of bounds, create a new function called wrap that requires one argument: the value of selection plus or minus 1, depending on which key was pressed. If that value would result in something less than 1 or higher than menmax, then reset selection to the lowest or highest value, as appropriate, and hand it back to the process that called the function. To save lazy programmers from too much typing, selection is renamed sel for use within this function.

As always, you can place this function anywhere in your code file.

```
function wrap(sel)
    if sel > menmax then
        sel = 1
    end
```

```
    if sel < 1 then
        sel = menmax
    end

    return sel
end
```

And finally, you must use this function when the arrow keys are pressed. Change the arrow key lines of your keypressed code.

```
function menu.keypressed(k)
    if k == "down" then
    selection = wrap(selection+1)
    elseif k == "up" then
    selection = wrap(selection-1)
```

Try your game now. You're able to select different menu items, and some even work. You can start a new game, and you can quit the application. You might notice that there's no way to get back to the menu once you've started a new game, but that's an easy fix. Add this code to you game.lua file:

```
function game.keypressed(k, uni)
    if k == "escape" then
        menu.activate()
    end
end
```

Try your application once more. Scroll through the menu, start a new game, return to the menu, and then quit. The first milestone has been reached: you have the framework that you need for a game and a menu system.

Git

As you have seen by now, there are times during development when an application just can't be launched, even for testing. Sometimes your code is incomplete, or sometimes you make some choices that render your project unusable. These are all important stages of development, and since it's through experimentation that most of the really good stuff gets done, it's not something you ever want to discourage in yourself. And yet, there's something significant about reaching an important milestone like the one you have just reached. Your project is in a pretty good state right now. Even though there's really not much to it, your current codebase serves as a solid foundation upon which the rest of the project can be built.

Furthermore, your project is divided into three files at the moment. If you had an assistant, you could save a lot of time by working on the game part and letting your assistant programmer work on the menu part. You'd probably both need access to `main.lua`, though, so eventually you'd have to come together and figure out what you each added or changed in each file, and then merge your combined work.

In the world of professional software development, this is known as *version control*, and the most popular version control system right now is Git.

Git was developed when Linus Torvalds and his fellow Linux kernel developers were ejected from a proprietary version control system, and suddenly found that they needed a way to manage lots of changes to hundreds of files between hundreds of developers. The lesson was clear: open source gives the users control of their own data and their own destiny. So, Torvalds developed his own system for managing code. Since then, Git is synonymous with software development. It's used by Linux, a huge portion of open source projects, Microsoft, Apple, and movie studios (i.e., Weta Digital, Sony, and Industrial Light & Magic), and it's the backbone of popular coding sites like GitLab and GitHub.

Git has no effect on your application; it's purely a tracking tool that enables you to maintain fluid backups and different development paths in one place. With Git, you get a running history of your project, with snapshots (called *commits* in Git terminology) of important moments in each file's life. This gives you the ability to (figuratively) go back in time and reverse mistakes you made along the way.

Learning Git is more a journey than a destination, but the sooner you start, the better. You already installed Git back when you installed Geany and several other tools, so it's ready to use.

Tracking

First, mark your code directory as a place you want Git to keep track of. You can do this in a terminal; first, change the directory to your project folder, and then run the git init command.

```
$ cd ~/battlejack
$ git init .
```

Alternatively, you can use a Git GUI called git-cola. This application is available from dnfdragora, but the latest version available at the time of this writing is included with the this book's source code. Install the latest version available from these two choices.

After you install git-cola, launch it from the applications menu or from a terminal.

```
$ git-cola &
```

The first window prompts you to select either a directory that is tracked by Git or (as in this case) a directory where you want to enable Git tracking. Click the New button and select your project folder. By selecting an untracked directory, you allow git-cola to enable Git tracking of that location.

In both cases, you can tell that Git tracking is enabled in a directory by listing the directory along with hidden files.

```
$ ls --all
./  ../  deck.ini  font/  game.lua  .git/  img/  main.lua
menu.lua
```

A directory being tracked by Git is usually called a *Git repository*, or a *Git repo* for short.

Adding Files

Git tracking is enabled for your project now, but Git only tracks what you tell it to track. You can see which files are (or are not) being tracked.

```
$ git status
On branch master
Initial commit
Untracked files:
  (use "git add <file>..." to include in what will be
  committed)
        deck.ini
        font/
        game.lua
        img/
        main.lua
        menu.lua
nothing added to commit but untracked files present (use "git
add" to track)
```

In git-cola, untracked files are listed in the Status pane.

Figure 7-2. *Untracked files in git-cola*

All files in the directory are currently untracked Figure 7-2. Since they're all in a healthy state (your game launches and you have code that you want to keep), add them all to Git using the wildcard character * as shorthand for *everything here.*

```
$ git add *
$ git status
On branch master
Initial commit
```

```
Changes to be committed:
  (use "git rm --cached <file>..." to unstage)
        new file:   deck.ini
        new file:   font/arkham.ttf
        new file:   game.lua
        new file:   img/red-10-wizard.png
        new file:   main.lua
        new file:   menu.lua
```

Now the files have been added to a special staging area. They've been marked for tracking, but you have yet to actually commit them. You can think of a Git commit as a sort of snapshot of the current state of a file. Commit everything in your staging area now.

```
$ git commit --message "game can switch between menu and game
screens"
[master (root-commit) 99dd051] game launches and switches
betwe[...]
 6 files changed, 46 insertions(+)
 create mode 100644 deck.ini
 create mode 100644 font/arkham.ttf
 create mode 100644 game.lua
 create mode 100644 img/red-10-wizard.png
 [...]
```

If you prefer to work within git-cola, add files by selecting them in the Status pane, and then right-click and select Stage Selected. This stages those files to be committed.

To commit all staged files, enter a commit message in the Commit pane, and then click the Commit button Figure 7-3.

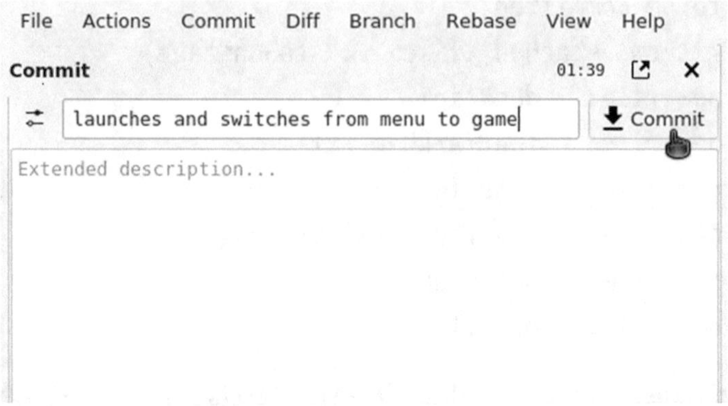

Figure 7-3. *Git commit in git-cola*

With your files committed, you can continue to develop with a peace of mind, knowing that if you ever get too far off track, you can always return to this point in your project's history.

Restoring

With everything safely committed to your Git repository, try breaking your project and then restoring from a previous commit.

First, change something arbitrary in game.lua to simulate some bad coding choices. Change this line

```
function game.new()
```

to this:

```
function game.run()
```

Now launch the game and try to start a new game. Previously, starting a new game shows a new screen, but now that you've made a bad edit, it crashes LÖVE.

Of course, in this example, the error is very small and easy to fix, but in the future, these kinds of problems will arise unintentionally, and after extensive changes have been made to several different files. The following reverts back to the most recent commit of a file in Git.

```
$ git checkout game.lua
```

Run your game now and start a new game. The game is back in working order.

If it's not just one file you need to revert, then you can reset your entire workspace back to the state of the most recent commit.

```
$ git reset --hard HEAD
```

To revert a file to the most recent commit using git-cola, find the changed file in the Modified section of the Status pane. Right-click it and select Revert Unstaged Edits.

You'll get a chance to do more with Git as you continue to work. The next logical step in your game's development is to focus on the part of the game that really matters: the game!

CHAPTER 8

Battling It Out

As of the previous chapter, both the menu and game screens are accessible when your program launches. In this chapter, you code the main game mechanics. The logic is similar to what you have already done to create your Blackjack game, so elements of this chapter will feel familiar, although there are unique features to Battlejack that pose new challenges.

The central game mechanic is this: like Blackjack, the goal is to reach 21 first. Unlike Blackjack, an excess of 21 is not a bust but still wins, and the player can "attack" the dealer's stash of cards.

During the game, the player clicks their deck to draw a card. On their turn, the player may select cards to cancel out a card in the AI's stash. This is an *attack*, and an attack may be bolstered by a powerup card if the player has one available. In the meantime, a player's cards are tallied for their own score in an attempt to reach 21 before the AI does. If the player draws a black card, then at the start of the dealer's turn, one black card from the player's hand is added to the dealer's stash.

If a joker is drawn from either deck, then it destroys the stash of the opposition.

In code, this game requires a lot of data tracking. Your code must keep track of what cards remain in each deck, what cards are in the player's hands, which of those cards are currently selected as cards to go into battle against the dealer, which cards are in the dealer's hand, which of the dealer's cards have been eliminated, the location of each card on the screen, and much more. In Lua terminology, that means you need tables ("classes" or "fields" in other languages).

© Seth Kenlon 2019
S. Kenlon, *Developing Games on the Raspberry Pi*,
https://doi.org/10.1007/978-1-4842-4170-7_8

Card Table

In your Blackjack game, each card was its own Lua table, with a unique `self.suit`, `self.value`, and `self.img` all its own, which you were able to call from your main script when you needed to calculate the total score or when you needed to tell LÖVE which image to draw on the screen.

Create a `card.lua` file in your project directory. This file is the card table: any time a card is generated for display on screen, it inherits all the attributes contained in this file. As you might expect, each card requires a face image and a numeric value and also a color. Each card also needs to keep track of its own location on the screen, which is useful in games because by updating one item's attributes, you can always restore or redraw the game state after major events.

```
Card = { }

function Card.init(c,v,f,x,y)
    -- generate card
    local self = setmetatable({}, Card)
    self.color = c
    self.value = v
    self.face  = f
    self.x = x
    self.y = y
    self.r = 0 --rotation

    return self
end
```

This is a slightly more complex version of your Blackjack card table. Of course, none of these values mean anything yet. They're just empty fields that need to be populated by data you feed into the table when generating a new card.

There are still a few more fields needed. First of all, each card needs an image. This would be identical to your Blackjack game were in not for the addition of the Joker to this deck. In fact, you could render the Joker and back images basically the same as all the other cards by naming their image files as you named the face cards (0-joker.png, 0-back.png) but then you need a copy of each in the red and black directories, which is redundant data. There's nothing wrong, necessarily, with that approach, but it wouldn't scale were this a much larger game with really big assets, while allowing for deviations in the code is cheap, and worthwhile.

Add this block of code above the return self line of your card.lua file:

```
if self.face == "back" or self.face == "joker" then
    self.img = love.graphics.newImage("img" .. d .. self.face
    .. ".png")
else
    self.img = love.graphics.newImage("img" .. d .. self.
    color .. d .. self.value .. "-" .. self.face .. ".png")
end
```

And finally, it's always important to be able to ascertain an object's size. A game object's size is vital for collision detection: it's how you tell where to draw the next object without drawing on top of the previous one, and it's how you detect whether the player has clicked one object or another.

Lua has functions specifically for the task of determining image size, but your program is going to scale your graphics down (as in the Blackjack game) so that the screen size can be changed. Technically, you could use Lua's size detection and multiply the result by your scale. Or, you can enter the size value as part of each card. Both do the same thing, but since the size of objects is used frequently, it's "cheaper" to do the calculation once and enter the value as a variable than to do the math every time a user interacts with the screen.

Add this above the `return self` line of your `card.lua` file:

```
self.wide = self.img:getWidth()*scale
self.high = self.img:getHeight()*scale
```

The value of the `scale` variable has yet to be created, but as long as it is defined before `card.lua` is actually used, there won't be a problem.

Game State

Currently, entering the game state of your application sets the active `STATE` to game, which in turn causes the main loop to invoke your custom `game.draw()` function, which renders a colored background. This all happens in the `game.lua` file, so open that in Geany so you can make some changes.

The `game.lua` file is the logical place to define important game-related variables, because it's within this file that the mechanics and game data tracking happens.

To begin with, the game logic needs access to your card class and to the configuration file that defines what cards exist. Add the top two lines of the following sample code to the top of your `game.lua` file.

```
require("card")
local inifile = require('inifile')
game = {}
```

If you have not already done so, use luarocks to install the `inifile` Lua library into your project directory.

```
$ cd ~/battlejack
$ luarocks install --tree=local inifile
```

Based on both the `card.lua` file and your previous experience with your Blackjack game, you can anticipate a few important variables that can be defined whether or not your code has a need for them yet.

Start by defining some environment variables. Eventually, LÖVE needs to know who is running the game so that it can store save files. Lua provides the os.getenv('HOME') function to discover a user's home directory. In Linux, this is a folder in a directory literally called home, whereas on the Mac, it is a folder within the Users directory, and on Windows it is a location usually on the C drive. The point is, you don't have to worry about where a user keeps their personal data files, because Lua finds that out for you.

Another thing that changes from system to system is the separator character used to delimit directories from one another. For instance, on the Raspberry Pi, as on any Linux or Mac system, the separator character is a forward slash. The location to any file or folder on the system can be predictably written out in plain text; for example, /home/ pi/battlejack/img/joker.png. On Windows, however, the separator character is traditionally a backslash: C:\\My Documents\example\img\ joker.png. Lua can detect this for you, too, with its package.config function.

Add the following lines to your game.lua file. The first line is already in your file and is shown for context.

```
game = {}

home = os.getenv('HOME')
d    = package.config:sub(1,1) -- path separator
```

Next, your game needs several tables to serve as decks of cards in various states of play. Create tables called hand and horde to serve as the player and AI active hands, tables called deck and ai to serve as shuffled draw decks for player and AI, a table called back containing the backside of the player and AI decks to serve as the clickable item when a player wants to draw a new card, and a grab table to serve as a staging area for cards a player is about to send into battle.

CHAPTER 8   BATTLING IT OUT

Finally, create a `winner` variable to mark whether or not a winner has been found. By default, set it to `nil`. Pull card data from your configuration file into a variable called `set` using the `inifile` function.

Here's the code you need to add. The first two lines are for context.

```
home = os.getenv('HOME')
d    = package.config:sub(1,1)
hand = {} --player hand
horde = {} --ai hand
deck = {} --player deck
ai   = {} --ai deck
back = {} --clickable deck icons
grab = {} --selected for battle
winner = nil

-- parse the INI file and
-- put values into a table called set
set = inifile.parse('deck.ini')
```

Your game world needs a `scale` variable to use when scaling down large card images to something that fits on the game screen. Since checking for the appropriate scale is something that has to be done any time a player changes the screen mode between windowed and fullscreen, setting the `scale` needs to be a function that can be called as necessary. Create a new function called `game.scaler()` in `game.lua` and use math to determine the optimal scale factor given the current size of the screen.

```
function game.scaler(WIDE,card)
    slot = WIDE/6
    scale = slot/card
    pad = WIDE*0.04
    return scale
end
```

The first logical place to call this function is any time a new game begins. The function takes the width of the screen, which is a global variable established in main.lua, and the native size of a card graphic. If you've made your own graphics for this game, then you must determine the size of your graphic yourself (you can find it in GIMP, if you're not sure). The example graphics included with the source code of this book are 790 pixels wide.

The game.scaler() function assumes that approximately six cards should fit horizontally across the screen (WIDE/6). This calculation renders the width of each card in pixels, which itself is important enough to keep in a global variable called slot, which keeps cards from overlapping when being drawn. The slot value divided by the unscaled size of a card provides a decimal number by which all cards may be scaled to fit six across the screen.

Add this line of code to your game.new() function:

```
scale = game.scaler(WIDE,790)
```

With these functions and variables in place, you can at least draw the most rudimentary of cards screen.

Setting the card table is an activity that needs to happen at the beginning of each new round, so it deserves its own function. Create one now, called game.setup(), and use your card library to generate cards to represent the player deck and the AI deck.

```
function game.setup()
    -- create GUI deck for player
    card = Card.init("c","v","back",pad,HIGH-slot-(pad*2))
    back[#back+1] = card
    -- create GUI deck for ai
    card = Card.init("c","v","back",WIDE-(slot/2)-pad,slot-(pad))
    back[#back+1] = card
```

```
-- draw table background
ground = love.graphics.newQuad(0,0,WIDE,HIGH,150,150)
tile   = love.graphics.newImage('img' .. d .. 'tile.jpg')
tile:setWrap('repeat','repeat')
end
```

The first card you generate is the "top" of the draw deck for the player. Since it's the back of a card, it has no color or value, so you pass in the "c" and "v" dummy values, which the card library ignores once it sees that the card being generated is of the back type. The card's X position is set at the left plus the value of pad, a variable set in main.lua to provide padding around the edges of the screen. The card's Y position is calculated from the height of the screen.

The card generated is added to the back table. Then the same variable is used to generate a second card to represent the AI's draw deck, using new X and Y values so that the card's placement is in the top right (across the virtual table) instead of the bottom left. This second card is also added to the back table.

Finally, a proper tabletop is defined. Currently, the game mode only renders a flat color in the background, but Battlejack deserves something more exciting. Rendering an array based on a texture or pattern is pretty common for a game engine, and LÖVE provides the love.graphics. newQuad function to map tiles across a given space. Specifically, this code defines a quad of the width and height of the screen, with tiles sized 150×150 pixels (which happens to be the size of the tile pattern included with the source code of this book). The tile is defined using the d variable to ensure compatibility with whatever system the game is running on, and the tile mode is set to wrap seamlessly across all available space.

Currently, nothing calls the game.setup() function, so trigger it at the end of the game.new() function, since a user starting a new game certainly expects their game to be set up.

```
game.setup()
```

Of course, nothing is actually drawn unless it appears in the love.
draw() function, which in this program is aliased to the draw() function of
whatever STATE the user is in. For game play, the user is in the game state,
so you must add your draw commands to game.draw().

Clear out the code currently in the game.draw() function, replacing it
with this:

```
function game.draw()
    love.graphics.setColor(1,1,1)

    -- set background
    love.graphics.draw(tile,ground,0,0)

    --hand player
    card = back[1]
    love.graphics.draw(card.img,card.x,card.y,0,scale,scale,0,0)
    --horde ai
    card = back[2]
    love.graphics.draw(card.img,card.x,card.y,0,-1*scale,-
    1*scale,card.img:getWidth()/2, card.img:getHeight()/2)
end
```

After setting the color to white to ensure that everything is drawn at
100% opacity, the tiles are drawn to create the tabletop. Order is important
here, so the tabletop must be drawn *before* cards are drawn, or else the
cards will be drawn "under" the table.

To draw the two card decks, you populate a temporary card variable
with one object from the back table and use that data to draw the graphic.
Since the back table contains relatively little data, manually pulling out an
entry is simple (the contents of the other tables that you have created are
far more dynamic and require for loops).

Launch your game to verify that all of your code is correct so far.
Correct any errors and make adjustments as needed, and then it's time to
set up the deck creation functions.

Deck Building

Like any card game, a key element of Battlejack is the random nature of the game elements. Functionally, that means your program needs a reliable set of methods that you can use repeatedly to create freshly randomized decks of cards based on the card definitions you have set forth in your card definition INI file.

To create decks for Battlejack, you must fill two distinct tables with card definitions: one filled with red cards and the other with black cards. However, it's part of the game design that there are six black "mole" cards inserted into the player deck, so six cards must be stolen from one deck and inserted into the other. Additionally, a Joker must be placed in each deck but not accidentally stolen when the black "mole" cards are inserted into the player deck. And finally, each deck must be shuffled to ensure unpredictability.

In your game.lua file, create four new functions: game.setsplit(), game.mole(), game.joker(), and game.shuffle().

First, to create two distinct tables containing card definitions for each color, you need to know which part of the INI file to use. For lack of better terminology, call this a *stack* (as in a stack of cards). You also need to know which deck you are building: red or black. Essentially, you need to determine whether the deck is meant for a human player or for the computer, so call this attribute *human*. Finally, you need a table to build the deck into, and you need to know the number of stacks to put into each deck, because it would be a very quick game were there only one copy of each card.

```
function game.setsplit(stack,human,tbl,n)
   for count = 1, n do
      for i,card in pairs(set[stack]) do
      if human == 1 then
         color="red"
```

```
    else
       color="black"
    end
    tbl[#tbl+1]=color .. "," .. card
      end
   end
   return tbl
end
```

This code uses a for loop to repeat the same action for as many times (n) as you proscribe when calling the function. The action that it takes is another for loop that iterates over the set variable, which contains the contents of the card section of your INI file, assigns a color to the card definition, and then places the card definition into whatever table you have told it to build into.

The table is returned at the end of the function, so you call the function as a constructor method, with its results placed into a destination of your choosing. For now, call the function in the game.setup() function.

```
-- create sets
deck = game.setsplit("card",1,deck,2)
ai   = game.setsplit("card",0,ai,2)
```

Next, you need to steal six cards from the black deck. If you do that immediately after building the decks, however, the same black cards are stolen every time because no randomness has been introduced into the decks. For this reason, you need to develop the shuffle method first.

As you might expect, asking a computer to do something randomly requires the use of Lua's math.random() function. This needs a random *seed*, and the easiest ever-changing source of numbers in a computer is its clock. Activate a random seed at the top of your game.new() function.

```
math.randomseed(os.time())
```

To cause a table to "shuffle" its order, you take the table into a function, determine the number of items it has in it, and then take a random number between 1 and the number of items in the table. Take the current item and swap it with the random numbered item. Repeat this until each item has traded places with some other item.

```
function game.shuffle(tbl)
    local len = #tbl
    for i = len, 1, -1 do
        local j = math.random( 1, i );
        tbl[i], tbl[j] = tbl[j], tbl[i];
    end
    return tbl;
end
```

Now that you have a way to shuffle decks, it's safe to steal cards from one to sabotage the other. For the game.mole() function, you first shuffle the AI deck to ensure that you're grabbing random cards. Then you take the first number of cards (the rules say six, but in case the function is used for some other purpose later, use n to signify a configurable number) and insert those cards into your target deck. Once inserted into the new deck, remove the stolen entry from the source table.

```
function game.mole(src,tgt,n)
    -- shuffle
    src = game.shuffle(src)

    for count = 1, n do
        tgt[#tgt+1] = src[count]
        table.remove(src,count)
    end
end
```

The last function inserts a Joker card into a deck. It's a straightforward table append.

```
function game.joker(tbl,human)
    if human == 1 then
        color="red"
    else
        color="black"
    end
    tbl[#tbl+1] = color .. ",joker,0"
    return tbl;
end
```

Now that the functions to build decks exist, you must use them. It's reasonable to first call these functions in the game.setup() function, since that is presumably called any time that a new game is started. Add this code to your setup:

```
-- create sets
deck = game.setsplit("card",1,deck,2)
ai = game.setsplit("card",0,ai,2)
-- steal cards from black
game.mole(ai,deck,6)
-- insert joker
deck = game.joker(deck,1)
ai   = game.joker(ai,0)
-- shuffle
deck = game.shuffle(deck)
ai = game.shuffle(ai)
```

If you launch your game now, it runs successfully but very quietly. For temporary insight into the inner workings of the game, add this block of code to the end of the setup() function:

```
print("deck ----------------")
for i,card in pairs(deck) do
    print(card)
end
print("ai ----------------")
for i,card in pairs(ai) do
    print(card)
end
```

Launch the game and look at the terminal to see a text list of the cards in each deck.

The next step is to transform all of this setup work into a playable game.

Playable Cards

Playing Battlejack is a three-step process: the user must draw a card, the user must select cards to use in an attack, and then the user must choose a target for an attack. That means your code needs functions to visually produce a card into the player's hand, to mark cards as selected, and finally, to resolve a battle.

Create a new function called game.cardgen() that accepts a deck as an argument. This function's job is to parse the next available card definition from a deck to use your card library to create a card object with all the necessary attributes (image, width, height, position, and so on), and to add it to the table representing the player's hand or the AI horde.

As cards are drawn from a deck, they must be removed from that deck or else the same card would be drawn for eternity. For that reason, the deck table becomes populated with nil entries as the game progresses, so your function must be programmed to skip over empty entries.

When a valid entry is found, the text must be parsed. Card data (as you were able to see when you wrote the temporary introspection for your last functions) is separated by commas; for example, black,goblin,5 or red,arcanist,3. To extract information from this, you use the Lua match function, which permits you to provide a *regular expression* representing the pattern of text you expect to see in each card entry of a deck. Specifically, you tell LÖVE to expect any text followed by a comma, and then any text followed by another comma, and finally, any text. Each component found by match is placed into a unique variable, which is passed to your card library.

```
function game.cardgen(src)
    local count = 0
    while src[count] == nil do count = count+1 end
    local c,f,v = src[count]:match("([^,]+),([^,]+),([^,]+)")
    card = Card.init(c,v,f,nil,nil)
    src[count] = nil

    if src == deck then
        hand[#hand+1] = card
        card.y = HIGH-(pad*2)-slot
    else
        horde[#horde+1] = card
        card.y = pad/4
    end
    return card
end
```

Now you need something to trigger your new function. Clicking the back of the player's deck should produce one card for the player, and one card for the AI. Unlike in your Blackjack game, there are several clickable objects in this game, so your mousereleased function needs to be able to detect exactly what clicked. This is best done with a dedicated click detection function that analyzes the X and Y coordinates of a click, compares it with the dimensions of some given object, and determines whether or not the X and Y of the click falls within the boundaries of the object.

```
function game.clicker(x,y,tgt)
    return (
        x < tgt.x + tgt.wide and
        x > tgt.x and
        y < tgt.y + tgt.high and
        y > tgt.y
    )
    -- returns True or False
end
```

Notice that this function is a little different than any of the functions you've written so far; it returns either true or false, depending on the results of its calculation. This is a convenience that lets you use the result of a call to the function as a sort of switch; if it returns false, then you know that there's no reason to continue analyzing a click.

Now when the player releases mouse button 1, look at both cards in the back table. Check whether either deck was clicked, but restrict the check to the lower half of the screen (rendering clicks in the AI deck meaningless). If so, generate one card for the player and one card for the AI.

```
function game.mousereleased(x,y,btn)
    if btn == 1 then
        --take a card
        for i,obj in pairs(back) do
        if game.clicker(x,y,obj) and y > HIGH-slot-pad then
            card = game.cardgen(deck)
            card = game.cardgen(ai)
        end --if
```

```
      end --for
   end --if
end
```

As usual, nothing is actually drawn to screen unless it's accounted for in the draw() function; so add two new for loops (one for each hand) to your draw loop. The first two lines are for context.

```
 -- set background
love.graphics.draw(tile,ground,0,0)

-- draw cards
for i,obj in pairs(horde) do --ai
   obj.x = WIDE-(slot*i)-slot-pad
   love.graphics.draw(obj.img,obj.x,obj.y,0,scale,scale,0,0)
end

for i,obj in pairs(hand) do --player
   obj.x = pad+(slot*i)
   love.graphics.draw(obj.img,obj.x,obj.y,obj.r,scale,scale,0,0)
end
```

Launch the game and draw some cards.

Battle

Sending cards into battle is also all about click detection. Since the user can select more than one card to combat an enemy card, you must mark selected cards as selected until an enemy target is clicked. You already have a table called grab, and so it serves as a kind of extension of the player's hand, containing any cards that have been clicked in preparation for battle. Of course, clicking an already grabbed card causes it to be deselected.

To detect whether a card is selected or not, you need a function to check for the presence of a specific card (the one that a player has clicked) in a table (the grab table). Create a function called game.isselected() and use it to cycle through a table in search of a specific card.

```
function game.isselected(src,tgt)
    for k,v in pairs(tgt) do
        if v==src then
        return k
        end
    end
end
```

Now that you have the ability to detect whether a card has been grabbed yet, you can process mouse clicks. For the action of grabbing a card and adding it to the grab table, you can use a the LÖVE mousepressed function, simply to avoid overloading the mousereleased function with too many checks.

The logic is simple. If mouse button 1 is pressed, check to see whether the object clicked is in the player's hand table. If it is, but it is not in the grab table, then change its position slightly to show that it is selected, and add it to the grab table. If it's already in the grab table, then move it back in line with the other cards and remove it from the table.

```
function love.mousepressed(x,y,btn)
    if btn == 1 then
        for i,obj in pairs(hand) do
        if game.clicker(x,y,obj) and not game.isselected(obj,grab)
        then
            obj.y = obj.y - (slot*2*scale)
            grab[#grab+1] = obj
        elseif game.clicker(x,y,obj) and game.isselected(obj,grab)
        > 0 then
```

```
        obj.y = HIGH-(pad*2)-slot
        k = game.isselected(obj,grab)
        grab[k] = nil
    end
      end
  end
end
```

Launch the game and try selecting some cards from your hand.

Visual Effects

Selecting cards for battle should be an exciting prospect in the game. After all, it's the central mechanic; without this, the game is basically Blackjack. While elevating the card on the table is pragmatically effective, it's not very flashy.

One way to "sweeten" the act of selecting cards for battle is to add a simple visual effect. You can imagine, for instance, that in a fantasy battle, warriors chosen to go out onto the front line might glow with a magical aura. In video game design terms, that translates to a particle effect.

Particle effects are relatively expensive, so you don't want to overuse them, especially on a relatively weak platform like the Pi. But as an indicator that something is "hot" and ready for battle, it's justified.

To set up a particle effect, you must point LÖVE to a graphic that is to be used as the actual particles. This particle serves as the raw material for the effect, and there are a few important attributes to set to keep the effect from devouring your processor and spreading particles all over the screen.

Add the following particle setup code to the top matter of your game. lua file. The first line is for context.

```
set = inifile.parse('deck.ini')

local mana = love.graphics.newImage('img' .. d .. 'part.png')
parti = love.graphics.newParticleSystem(mana, 12)
parti:setParticleLifetime(2,5) -- Particles live span min,max
parti:setEmissionRate(4)
parti:setSizeVariation(1)
parti:setLinearAcceleration(-12,-12,12,0) --xmin,ymin,xmax,ymax
parti:setColors(255,255,255,255,255,255,255,0) --Fade
```

To use the effect, add it to your draw function. Its placement is important, since you probably want it to be rendered *under* the player cards so that the particles appear to be rising up from within or behind the selected cards.

```
for i,obj in pairs(grab) do
   local count = 1
   while count < obj.wide/mana:getWidth() do
      love.graphics.draw(parti,obj.x+(mana:getWidth()*count+1),
      obj.y+(pad/3))
      count = count+1
   end
end

for i,obj in pairs(hand) do -- this line for context
```

Since the particle graphic itself is quite small, this code uses a while loop to place a particle seed along the top edge of any card in the grab table.

Finally, use the LÖVE update function to detect and update changes in the particles. It only needs to take action if the grab table is not empty.

```
function love.update(dt)
   if #grab > 0 then
      parti:update(dt)
   end
end
```

Launch your game again and select some cards for battle to see the effect Figure 8-1.

Figure 8-1. *Particle effects used to highlight a selection*

Resolving Conflict

To settle the outcome of a card battle, you must compare the player's cards selected for battle against the AI card being targeted. This happens only if 1 or more cards is present in the grab table, and only when a card in the AI horde has been clicked.

There's also one important exception to any attack: if the card is a Joker, then *all* cards in the horde are wiped out.

To obliterate an entire hand, you can use a new function. Call it game. blast() and make it clear out whatever table it is provided.

```
function game.blast(tgt)
   local count = #tgt
   for i=0, count do tgt[i]=nil end
end
```

This function is useful not only for a Joker attack, but also as a way to make sure a player is starting with an empty hand, horde, grab, and other tables, at the start of a new game. In fact, why not add summary blasts to the game.new() function now.

```
function game.new()
   game.blast(deck)
   game.blast(ai)
   game.blast(hand)
   game.blast(horde)
   game.blast(back)
   game.blast(grab)
   winner   = nil

   scale = game.scaler(WIDE,790)
```

```
-- start new game
STATE = game
math.randomseed(os.time())

game.setup()
end
```

If you launch your game and draw a few cards, and then press Esc to bring up the menu, and then start a new game, you find that a new game is now, finally, truly a new game.

Resolving battle is still incomplete. Aside from the blast function, it mostly happens within the mousereleased function.

Order is important now. Currently, your mousereleased function checks whether the mouse button is button 1 and then takes action. But the button is always button 1, so new qualifiers are required. For instance, if the mouse button is 1 and there are cards currently grabbed, then check to see if it was a card in the horde table that was clicked. If so, then it's time to battle. If not, then check that the click was button 1 and that a card in the back table was clicked, and draw a card.

In addition to removing the attacked horde cards, the player's resources require adjustment. The cards used in the attack are also removed from the player hand. However, this must only happen if the attack is successful, since a player could attempt to attack without enough power to actually remove cards from the field. You must decide through play testing whether a successful attack must be greater than a black card, or if a card that is equal to or greater than a black card is victorious. The sample code here allows for cards both equal in value and greater in value to defeat the opponent.

Create a new function called game.postbattle() to perform the menial task of removing cards from a table.

```lua
function game.postbattle(src,tgt)
   for i,card in ipairs(src) do --remove grabbed cards
      k = game.isselected(card,src)
      src[k] = nil
      k = game.isselected(card,tgt)
      table.remove(tgt,k)
   end
end
```

And then perform the checks and balances of battle in the mousereleased function.

```lua
function game.mousereleased(x,y,btn)
   local attack = 0

   if btn == 1 and #grab > 0 then
      for i,obj in pairs(horde) do      --examine each card in
      horde
      if game.clicker(x,y,obj) then --get horde card that got
      clicked

         for i,card in pairs(grab) do --check value of grabbed
         cards
            attack >= attack+tonumber(card.value) --add value to
            total attack

            if card.face == "joker" then
          game.blast(horde)
          game.postbattle(grab,hand)
            end --if
         end --for
```

```
    if attack > tonumber(obj.value) then
        -- remove from horde
        k = game.isselected(obj,horde)
        table.remove(horde,k)
        game.postbattle(grab,hand)
    end --if
  end
   end
elseif btn == 1 then
   --take a card
   for i,obj in pairs(back) do
   if game.clicker(x,y,obj) and y > HIGH-slot-pad then
      card = game.cardgen(deck)
      card = game.cardgen(ai)
   end --if
    end --for
  end --elseif
end
```

Launch your game and take out the opposition. There's no win or lose condition yet, and there may be a few crashes, but the basic mechanic and game play is complete. Your game is now firmly in alpha.

CHAPTER 9

Balance of Power

There are a few small bugs in Battlejack, and a few opportunities for a better user experience. This chapter fixes the bugs and adds some features to make the game flow better.

The first bug you may not have noticed yet: if you click the mouse on the menu screen, the game crashes. This is caused by the main.lua file forwarding any detected mouse press or release to STATE.mousepressed() or STATE.mousereleased(), and finding no corresponding menu.mousepressed() or menu.mousereleased() function.

The fix is simple: create functions to process mouse events on the menu screen. Since no action is required on a mouse event, a dummy response is all that's needed.

```
function menu.mousereleased(x,y,btn)
    return false
end

function menu.mousepressed(x,y,btn)
    return false
end
```

Another noticeable bug is the lack of feedback from the game. The progress of the game is very difficult to follow without a running tally of each player's score, and without the declaration of who has won and who has lost.

© Seth Kenlon 2019
S. Kenlon, *Developing Games on the Raspberry Pi*,
https://doi.org/10.1007/978-1-4842-4170-7_9

To print the current totals of each hand, you must calculate a running total that updates as frequently as each hand changes. The two functions that update most frequently are the draw() and update(dt) functions, and there's not necessarily any reason to use one over the other. However, since the draw() function is busy drawing cards and hands, put the calculation in the update function.

For context, the whole update function is as follows.

```
function love.update(dt)
    if #grab > 0 then
        parti:update(dt)
    end
    handval=0
    hordeval=0
    for i,obj in pairs(hand) do
        handval = handval+tonumber(obj.value)
    end
    for i,obj in pairs(horde) do
        hordeval = hordeval+tonumber(obj.value)
    end
end
```

Notice that the values of handval and hordeval are each reset at the beginning of each update. This ensures that the total score is recalculated with every update rather than compounded upon itself. The total for each hand is the sum of each card in each hand, using the tonumber Lua method to translate the value of each card from a string into an integer.

Drawing the tally on screen is done the same way as drawing any text on screen, and for added effect you can add a graphical element to suggest a magical glow. Sample graphics are included in the code files for this book.

Create the effect graphics for each deck near the top of your game.lua file.

```
local glow = love.graphics.newImage('img' .. d .. 'glow.png')
local shadow = love.graphics.newImage('img' .. d .. 'shadow.png')
```

Then add the graphics and running total to your game.draw() function. The draw function is getting crowded, and order does matter for layering effects, so here is the complete function so far.

```
function game.draw()
    love.graphics.setColor(1,1,1)
    -- set background
    love.graphics.draw(tile,ground,0,0)
    --hand player
    font = love.graphics.setNewFont("font/Arkham_reg.TTF",36)
    card = back[1]
    love.graphics.draw(glow,card.x,card.y-(card.y/4),0,scale,
    scale,0,0)
    love.graphics.draw(card.img,card.x,card.y,0,scale,scale,0,0)
    love.graphics.setColor(0,0,0)
    love.graphics.printf(tostring(handval),(slot)-slot/2,card.y-
    pad,slot/2,'center')
    love.graphics.setColor(1,1,1)
    --horde ai
    card = back[2]
    love.graphics.draw(shadow,card.x,(card.y*2)+card.y/2,0,
    scale,scale,card.img:getWidth()/2, card.img:getHeight()/2)
    love.graphics.draw(card.img,card.x,card.y,0,-1*scale,-
    1*scale,card.img:getWidth()/2, card.img:getHeight()/2)
    love.graphics.setColor(0.8,0.1,0.1)
```

```
love.graphics.printf(tostring(hordeval),card.x-pad,card.
y+card.y,slot/2,'center')
love.graphics.setColor(1,1,1)
font = love.graphics.setNewFont("font/Arkham_reg.TTF",72)

-- draw cards
for i,obj in pairs(horde) do --ai
   obj.x = WIDE-(slot*i)-slot/2
   love.graphics.draw(obj.img,obj.x,obj.y,0,scale,scale,0,0)
end
for i,obj in pairs(grab) do
   local count = 1
   while count < obj.wide/mana:getWidth() do
   love.graphics.draw(parti,obj.x+(mana:getWidth()*
   count+1),obj.y+(pad/3))
   count = count+1
   end
end
for i,obj in pairs(hand) do --player
   obj.x = pad+(slot*i)
   love.graphics.draw(obj.img,obj.x,obj.y,obj.r,scale,
   scale,0,0)
end
end
```

Try playing the game now to test the new functions, taking note of bugs or missing features.

Git Commit

A lot of progress has been made up to this point, so it makes sense to commit the changes to Git, just in case changes you make later render the game unplayable by mistake.

Open git-cola and look in the Status pane to see which files you have changed but not yet committed. A Git *commit* is like a snapshot, so even though you have committed an earlier version of a file, you must take a new snapshot of any changes since the original commit.

You can also review your Git repository in a terminal.

```
$ cd ~/battlejack
$ git status
On branch master
Changes not staged for commit:
  (use "git add <file>..." to update what will be committed)

  modified:   game.lua
  modified:   menu.lua
no changes added to commit (use "git add" and/or "git commit -a")
```

In git-cola, right-click the updated files in the Status pane and select "Stage selected".

Or in a terminal, enter the following.

```
$ git add game.lua menu.lua
```

To commit the files to Git with git-cola, fill in a brief commit message and then click the Commit button. To do the same in the terminal.

```
$ git commit -m 'click interception and running total score'
```

In the future, you should commit code whenever you make a significant change that has not broken your codebase. It's a good habit to get into, and in case of disaster, it can save you hours of work.

Leveling Up

Game difficulty is a tricky to get right. What's gratifyingly difficult for one player is discouraging to another, so the level of challenge in your game is ultimately up to you. However, playing through the game as it is now, it's arguable that the Joker card in both decks is imbalanced. For the player, it buys valuable time as the AI brute forces its way toward a winning hand, but it would be a guaranteed loss for the player should a Joker be played against them. For that reason, comment out the addition of a Joker card to the AI deck.

```
deck = game.joker(deck,1)
--ai   = game.joker(ai,0)
```

That balances the game, and catching it early prevents you from having to write the code associated with the AI playing a Joker card. If you decide to add it back later because you *want* the extra challenge, you can use the game.blast function when the player draws a Joker card, and you can write the necessary code.

Balancing a game isn't just crippling the opposition, but also bolstering the player. The human player in Battlejack is up against a relentless march of cards that are drawn but never spent. Tipping the scales in the player's favor has two important effects: it makes the player feel more powerful as they achieve victories, and it assures the player that all their hard work is paying off.

To create a leveling system, instantiate a variable at the top of game.lua, setting it to 0 by default. The first line in the code sample is for context.

```
winner = nil
level  = 0
```

The level can be printed on screen using the usual love.graphics.printf function, which you've already used in both Blackjack and Battlejack. However, the player doesn't really need a constant reminder of what level they're on, so it's a good idea to create some marker variable to signal the level text to disappear. You could use the Lua os.clock function to measure the passage of time, but in a turn-based game like Battlejack, time is more or less relative compared to when the player clicks, so it's more meaningful to use clicks as a measure of "time" than actual time.

Create a new variable called progress to represent how far into a game the player has progressed. This variable needs to be reset each time a new game is started, so create and set the variable in the game.new function.

```
progress = 0
```

Increment the variable whenever the mouse is released. The first two lines are for context.

```
function game.mousereleased(x,y,btn)
    local attack = 0
    progress = progress+1
```

And finally, in the draw function, draw the level text until progress is 2 or greater.

```
if progress < 2 then
    love.graphics.printf("Level " .. level,0,pad+HIGH/3,WIDE,
    'center')
end
```

To increment a level, you need a way to determine the winner. You wrote similar code for the Blackjack game, and it only needs minor adjustment for this game. Here is the complete update function.

```
function love.update(dt)
    if #grab > 0 then
        parti:update(dt)
    end
```

```
   handval=0
   hordeval=0
   for i,obj in pairs(hand) do
      handval = handval+tonumber(obj.value)
      if obj.color == "bonus" then
    handval = handval-tonumber(obj.value)
      end
   end
   for i,obj in pairs(horde) do
      hordeval = hordeval+tonumber(obj.value)
   end
   -- ID the winner
   if handval >= 21 and handval > hordeval then
      winner = "hand"
   elseif hordeval >= 21 and hordeval > handval then
      winner = "horde"
   elseif handval >= 21 and handval == hordeval then
      winner = "tie"
   end
end
```

Each mouse release, check to see whether a winner has been declared and either increment the level or start a new round. This check must be performed before anything else so that as soon as there's a valid winner, game play stops.

The first three lines are for context.

```
function game.mousereleased(x,y,btn)
local attack = 0
progress = progress+1
```

```
if btn == 1 and winner ~= nil then
   if winner == "hand" then
   level = level+1
end
   game.sleep(1)
   game.new()
end
```

This code refers to a new function that doesn't exist yet: game.sleep. This function causes the game to "sleep" to ensure that the player isn't missing important information. Without a brief pause, the game would go from "You win" to "Level 1" messages in the blink of an eye.

Unlike many programming languages, there is no function in Lua's standard library for sleeping, but it's an easy function to implement. Add this to game.lua:

```
function game.sleep(s)
   local ntime = os.clock() + s
   repeat until os.clock() > ntime
end
```

You can play the game now to see the latest improvements. Remember to commit your changes with Git, as long as everything works as expected.

Powerup

The game increases the player's levels but so far doesn't actually reward them with anything substantial. Now that the level mechanism is in place, you can use it to add new cards into the player's deck any time they gain a level. This gives the player the feeling of growing power, and a sense of accomplishment.

First, you need some way to alert the player of their accomplishment. You could print a message on the game screen, but for something as significant as an hard-earned powerup, a special message screen seems more important and means less clutter in the game play area.

On the message screen, you can display the new cards added to the deck after each victory. It can do double duty as an alert message when the player draws a black card from their own deck, underscoring that their luck has changed for the worst.

You need a few new tables and variables for this mechanism. Since there are sets of cards involved, you need new tables, earn for earned bonuses and up for powerups. Since the winner variable is set back to nil with each new game, you need a new persistent variable called lastwon to represent whether the player won the last round or not.

You also need to create a new file called msg.lua to serve as your message screen.

Add these new elements to the top of your game.lua file.

```
require("card")
require("msg")

up     = {} --powerups
earn  = {} --earned bonuses
winner = nil
level   = 0
lastwon = 0
```

In a new file called msg.lua, build a new game state called msg. This is similar to the menu game state. When activated, the STATE variable changes to msg, meaning all user input is directed to msg.lua, meaning you need the same mouse click interception as other modes. Since the point of this message screen is to convey information to the player, create an OK button to dismiss the screen.

```
msg = {}

function msg.activate()
   STATE = msg
   font = love.graphics.setNewFont("font/Junction_regular.
   otf",24)
   button_ok = love.graphics.newImage("img" .. d ..
   "button_ok.png")
end

function msg.mousereleased(x,y,btn)
   return false
end

function msg.keypressed(k)
   game.activate()
end
```

You also need a function to detect clicks made on the OK button, and a mouse click function to respond to those clicks. It's arbitrary, in this case, whether you respond to a mouse press or a mouse release, since in either case the result is the dismissal of the message screen and the activation of the game state.

```
function msg.clicker(x,y,tgt)
   return (
     x < (WIDE/2)-(button_ok:getWidth()/2) + tgt:getWidth()
     and
       x > (WIDE/2)-(button_ok:getWidth()/2) and
   y < HIGH/2 + tgt:getHeight() and
       y > HIGH/2
   )
   -- returns True or False
end
```

```
function msg.mousepressed(x,y,btn)
   if btn == 1 and msg.clicker(x,y,button_ok) then
      game.activate()
   end
end
```

And finally, you must generate the content of the message. Since the message screen is going to serve as an alert for bonuses and powerups as well as the unfortunate instance of drawing a black card from the player deck, you must use an if statement to determine whether you need to display two cards (a bonus and a powerup) or just one card (a single black card drawn from the player deck).

```
function msg.draw()
   love.graphics.setBackgroundColor(0.1,0.1,0.1)
   if earncard ~= nil then
      love.graphics.draw(upcard.img,((WIDE-upcard.wide)/2)-
      upcard.wide,pad,0,scale,scale,0,0)
      love.graphics.draw(earncard.img,(WIDE+earncard.
      wide)/2,pad,0,scale,scale,0,0)
   else --only one card to display
      love.graphics.draw(upcard.img,((WIDE-upcard.wide)/2),pad,
      0,scale,scale,0,0)
   end
   love.graphics.printf(message,0,pad+HIGH/3,WIDE,'center')

   love.graphics.draw(button_ok, (WIDE/2)-(button_ok:getWidth()
   /2),HIGH/2,0,1,1,0,0)
end
```

This introduces two new variables: an earncard and an upcard. These variables don't exist yet, but you will create them before calling the new msg screen. They will contain the card or cards that have been generated from either a victory or an unfortunate hand.

As with the card sets for your player and AI, you must populate your earned bonus and powerup tables in the game.setup() function.

```
up = game.setsplit("up",1,up,1)
earn = game.setsplit("earn",1,earn,1)
```

You also need a method for inserting new cards into the player's deck. You have already created a method to insert a Joker card into a deck, and while it seemed like a sensible function at the time, you can see now that it could be expanded into a generic method for inserting any card type into a deck. An additional argument is required so that the function can differentiate between a normal card and a bonus or powerup card, and the function name should change to better reflect its new generic purpose.

Change the game.joker function to this:

```
function game.adder(tbl,human,card,v,bonus)
    if bonus == 1 then
        color="bonus"
    elseif bonus == 0 and human == 1 then
        color="red"
    else
        color="black"
    end
    tbl[#tbl+1] = color .. "," .. card .. "," .. tostring(v)
    return tbl;
end
```

Accordingly, change the Joker addition to the player deck in the game. setup function.

```
deck = game.adder(deck,1,"joker",0,0)
```

And then add the bonus and powerup cards to the deck. These cards are only added after level 0 has been won, and the player is only alerted to new additions that have been won from the previous victory.

Once the cards have been earned, they are silently added to the deck. This means that a message screen is only shown when lastwon is set to 1. It also means that which cards are added can be controlled according to the current value of the level variable. That is, starting at level 1, all cards in the earn and up tables, from 1 to 1, are added. At level 2, all cards from 1 to 2 are added. At level 3, all cards from 1 to 3 are added, and so on. When you have no further cards to add, the limit is capped to the highest number of cards defined in the earn and up sets of deck. ini.

Add the following code to your game.setup function. The first two and last two lines are for context.

```
deck = game.adder(deck,1,"joker",0,0)
--ai = game.adder(ai,0,"joker",0)

-- power ups
if level > 0 then
   local limit = level
   if level > 8 then limit = 8 end
   for i = 1, limit, 1 do
 c,f,v = up[i]:match("([^,]+),([^,]+),([^,]+)")
   deck = game.adder(deck,1,f,v,1)
   end
   upcard = Card.init("bonus",v,f,WIDE/2,HIGH/2)

   -- earned bonuses
   local limit = level
   if level > 5 then limit = 5 end
   for i = 1, limit, 1 do
 c,f,v = earn[i]:match("([^,]+),([^,]+),([^,]+)")
   deck = game.adder(deck,1,f,v,0)
   end
   earncard = Card.init(c,v,f,WIDE/2,HIGH/2)
```

```
  --alert player if recent win
  if lastwon == 1 then
 message="New cards added to your deck!"
 msg.activate(earncard,upcard,message)
  end
end

-- shuffle
deck = game.shuffle(deck)
ai = game.shuffle(ai)
```

The alert mechanism requires that lastwon is kept updated across rounds. It is only set to 1 when the player has just won a round. It is set to 0 in a loss or a tie. Add lastwon management to the game.draw function code that monitors for a winner. Most of the following code exists in your function already, so only add the lastwon lines to your existing code.

```
if winner == "hand" then
   lastwon = 1
   love.graphics.printf("You have won!",0,pad+HIGH/3,WIDE,
   'center')
elseif winner == "horde" then
   lastwon = 0
   love.graphics.printf("You have lost.",0,pad+HIGH/3,WIDE,
   'center')
elseif winner == "tie" then
   lastwon = 0
   love.graphics.printf("Tied game.",0,pad+HIGH/3,WIDE,
   'center')
end
```

The other purpose for the message screen is to alert the player when a traitor has been discovered among their ranks, or in mechanical terms, they have drawn a black card from their own red deck.

This requires an if statement in the game.mousereleased function, when a new card is drawn from the player deck. When a card is generated, you assign it to the card variable, and since card generation uses your own card.lua code, you know that you can look at its color by looking at card.color. If the color is black, then you can trigger a few actions. First, a message should be given to the player, telling them of the bad news. Then, the card must be placed into the AI hand and removed from its default destination of the player's hand.

Adjust the final elseif clause in your game.mousereleased function.

```
elseif btn == 1 then
   --take a card
   for i,obj in pairs(back) do
  if game.clicker(x,y,obj) and y > HIGH-slot-pad then
     card = game.cardgen(deck)
     if card.color == "black" then
        -- insert card into horde
        card.y = pad/4
        horde[#horde+1] = card
        message="Black card drawn!"
        earncard = nil
        upcard   = card
        msg.activate()
        -- remove card from hand
        hand[#hand] = nil
```

Try playing a few rounds to see how the new bonus and powerup cards perform.

Powerup Double Draw

Now that the game is more complex and more complete, play testing is a little difficult. You have to play longer, and press more keys or click more things to find the bugs. Don't let that deter you, though; there are bugs to fix yet.

One notably missing feature is the way powerup cards are treated. First of all, they're counting toward the total of the player's hand, but they're meant to be powerups, not just another card. Contrariwise, the powerup cards count as one card draw, meaning that in a sense they penalize the player because the game's most urgent mechanic is the need for more cards. If a "powerup" card takes up a turn but adds nothing to the player's points stash, then the player is arguably better off without the powerup.

The way to make a powerup feel like a powerup is to give the player a second card any time a powerup card is drawn. That way, a powerup card adds temporary ammunition to the player's hand but doesn't cost them any points toward their score.

Add the following exemption to the score calculation in the update function.

```
handval=0
hordeval=0
for i,obj in pairs(hand) do
    handval = handval+tonumber(obj.value)
    if obj.color == "bonus" then
        handval = handval-tonumber(obj.value)
    end
end
```

And then add a free additional card draw whenever a bonus card is detected in the game.draw function. This requires an additional elseif clause at the end of the final if code. The first line and last five lines are for context (and are marked as such).

```
      hand[#hand] = nil --context
   elseif card.color == "bonus" then
     card = game.cardgen(deck)
     if card.color == "black" then
        -- insert card into horde
        card.y = pad/4
        horde[#horde+1] = card
        hand[#hand] = nil
     end
   end
   card = game.cardgen(ai) --context
   end
  end
 end --if
end
```

The logic here is fairly simple, but for the one exception when a player draws a bonus card and then a black card. The code first checks for a bonus card. If the card is a bonus card, then a new card is immediately drawn. If that card is a black card, then that card is silently moved into the AI's hand and removed from the player's hand. This is done without a message to avoid too many alerts. You can change this, if you prefer verbosity, but during play testing pay close attention to how often the game is interrupted so that you don't annoy your players.

Font and UI Consistency

There's another bug hidden in the code that you might not have discovered yet. Because the game uses two different fonts and font sizes, going back to the menu screen after a game has started results in unreadable menu options. The fix for this is to monitor font settings closely. Specifically, you can enforce the "default" font for each game state in the `activate` functions.

184

For instance, the only font needed for the menu state is the rather plain Junction font at 14 points. Make sure that the `font` variable is set to that every time the menu is activated.

```
function menu.activate()
    STATE = menu
    selection = 1
    font = love.graphics.setNewFont("font/Junction_regular.
    otf",14)
end
```

Similarly, the primary font for the game state is the stylish Arkham font at 72 points.

```
function game.activate()
    -- switch to game screen
    STATE = game
    font = love.graphics.setNewFont("font/Arkham_reg.TTF",72)
end
```

And the message screen uses plain old Junction, for readability. This should already exist in your code, but confirm that your `msg.activate` function is as follows.

```
function msg.activate()
    STATE = msg
    font = love.graphics.setNewFont("font/Junction_regular.
    otf",24)
    button_ok = love.graphics.newImage("img" .. d .. "button_
    ok.png")
end
```

This resolves any inconsistencies in the user interface.

Garbage Collection

The final bug to squash is a rather serious crash that you only see after several rounds. The crash renders an *out of memory* error, which is caused by the vast amounts of data being moved in and out of this game. This is a niche problem caused by this type of game; usually, Lua is fully capable of managing memory, but with all the cards and graphics that Battlejack cycles through, it's difficult for Lua to know what information we expect to have access to.

Part of memory management is called garbage collection. Most modern programming languages have it built in, although some low-level languages like C and C++ do not. Although built upon C, Lua has automated garbage collection but allows for manual memory management when needed.

Garbage collection, as its name suggests, is a signal you can send to Lua to assure it that it's safe to cycle through old variables and clear them from memory. There are a few places that you can expect this to be safe: at the beginning of a new game, there's certainly no reason to keep information from previous rounds, and when the player uses the Joker card, which only happens once per round, it can be safely assumed that very old data is no longer required. This is mostly guess work, of course; you have no way of monitoring exactly what Lua is keeping track of in the recesses of its memory allotment, but the Lua collectgarbage() function is a trigger for Lua to run a garbage collection cycle sooner than its default schedule. You're still leaving it up to Lua to decide what to remove from memory, and Lua is smart enough to know that, for instance, the lastwon variable is still important and must *not* be erased, while the structure of the previous decks are safe to discard.

Add a collectgarbage() flag to the game.new() function.

```
function game.new() --for context
collectgarbage()
game.blast(deck)      --for context
And when a Joker is used:
```

```
if card.face == "joker" then
   game.blast(horde)
   game.postbattle(grab,hand)
   collectgarbage()    --added
end
```

For most Lua programs, you won't run into memory management problems. However, if you do, you now know how to prompt Lua to review its resources and clear out unused data.

Homework

The game, strictly speaking, is now complete. There are a few features, like save files and screen size, implemented in the next chapter, but otherwise, game play is smooth and (ideally) bug free. Here are a few things to look at between now and the next chapter:

- Before moving on, commit your changes to Git.

- Play a few rounds of Battlejack to get a feel for difficulty. Is it challenging enough? Is it too difficult? What adjustments can you make?

- You can leverage your new level system to adjust difficulty. For instance, you might want to start the game with fewer traitor cards in the red deck, and then ramp up the number as the player progresses.

  ```
  if level >= 4 and level < 6 then
      game.mole(ai,deck,4)
  elseif level >= 6
      game.mole(ai,deck,6)
  else
      game.mole(ai,deck,2)
  end
  ```

- Or you might want to do the opposite, such that the game appears to become easier as the player progresses. This is an alternate theory of game design, in which to give the player the illusion of increasing power, you "nerf" the enemies.

```
if level < 2 then
    game.mole(ai,deck,6)
else
    game.mole(ai,deck,4)
end
```

- Try the game again to see how it progresses.

- Think of some other ways to help the balance of power in Battlejack and try them out.

- It's not easy, but it is possible to exhaust a full deck with no winner or loser. There's no code to handle this event, so the game crashes.

- Invent a reliable way for the game to respond to empty draw decks. There are several ways to do this. You could declare a winner based on the state of the game when the decks are exhausted (closest to 21 wins). You could hold a final death-match to decide the winner, in which the player and AI each draw a card from a fresh deck; the best card wins. Or you could just create fresh decks and continue the game seamlessly.

CHAPTER 10

Save Files and Game States

The Battlejack game is fully functional, but there are still convenience functions to add, including saving and loading game progress, and switching between fullscreen and windowed mode.

Realistically, Battlejack doesn't exactly demand a fullscreen mode, since it's a relatively simple game. But for more complex games with a complex story, you might want to encourage immersion, and one way to help the player focus on the game and only the game is to give them the option for the game to take over their entire screen.

The problem with switching between fullscreen and windowed mode is that the graphic sizes must be recalculated. You may even see, in some games, that changing the resolution of the game requires the game to be relaunched before it can redraw. LÖVE can change dimension dynamically, as long as your code adjusts for the change.

Fullscreen

In its current state, your Battlejack code requires some changes to account for a sudden change in game window size. If you're not a fan of math, many of the changes will seem a little mysterious, but the most important concept is the use of relative measurements. You must base

© Seth Kenlon 2019
S. Kenlon, *Developing Games on the Raspberry Pi*,
https://doi.org/10.1007/978-1-4842-4170-7_10

the size of game elements on the width and height of the user's current window size, but in order to do that you must ask the user's system what that size is. In practice, this often means that you have to adjust the location of elements to account for a potential change in empty (or "negative") space.

The first file that needs an update is the place where fullscreen mode is toggled on and off: the menu screen. There are a few LÖVE functions that deal with window sizes.

```
love.window.getFullscreen()
```

Whether or not the current window is in fullscreen mode. This function returns a Boolean value: `true` or `false`.

```
love.window.setFullscreen()
```

Activates fullscreen mode.

```
love.window.getMode()
```

Returns the mode of the window.

```
love.window.setMode()
```

Sets the window dimensions.

```
love.window.updateMode()
```

Forces the window to update its mode settings.

With these functions, you can always determine whether your game screen is fullscreen or windowed, and extract the dimensions of the space you have available.

The fullscreen toggle selection in menu.lua is option 3 (it's the third selection in the menu entries array). Currently, there's a placeholder there: it returns true, which in this context is Lua shorthand for *not an error*.

Erase the placeholder and fill in some useful logic to determine whether the window is currently in fullscreen mode. If it is not in fullscreen, place it in fullscreen mode and get the dimensions of the screen so that the variables WIDE and HIGH have accurate numbers in them for use by calculations in the game code. If the window is currently in fullscreen mode, set the width and height back to the default size. In either case, update the mode to make sure that LÖVE forces a redraw of the entire window.

```
elseif selection == 3 then
    if not love.window.getFullscreen() then
        love.window.setFullscreen(true, "desktop")
        WIDE,HIGH = love.window.getMode()
    else
        WIDE,HIGH = 960,720
        love.window.setMode(WIDE,HIGH)
    end
    love.window.updateMode(WIDE,HIGH,{resizable=true,
    vsync=false,minwidth=WIDE,minheight=HIGH})
    fsupdated = 1
```

At the end of this code, a new variable called fsupdated is created and set to 1. This variable serves as a flag signaling that the window mode has been changed, which in turn lets you write code in game.lua that only runs when a window mode change is made.

For the game to resize, several adjustments are required. Some game elements in Battlejack have been purposefully misconfigured in earlier chapters so that you can see the difference between a reasonable first attempt and, ultimately, the correct code. The important thing to understand is that when scaling a game, you must think about many different factors, and these factors may be unique to your game, depending on the assets you use. The examples in this section are specific to

Battlejack, but the principles of using variables for calculations, detecting changes in screen settings, and knowing what can and cannot scale, are broadly applicable no matter what your game is like.

Open game.lua for editing. The various states of the game are defined by the variable STATE. Any time a user enters game mode, it is by triggering the game.activate function, whether by selecting New game or pressing Esc. That means that any time a user is in the menu screen, the game.activate function is the entry point to the game, and the ideal place to detect whether the screen size has changed.

Change game.activate() function to match this code.

```
function game.activate()
    -- switch to game screen
    STATE = game
    ground = love.graphics.newQuad(0,0,WIDE,HIGH,150,150)
    font = love.graphics.setNewFont("font/Arkham_reg.TTF",72)

    if fsupdated == 1 then
        scale = game.scaler(WIDE,790)

        local arr = {hand,horde,back,grab}
        for i,tbl in ipairs(arr) do
      for n,obj in pairs(tbl) do
          obj.wide = obj.img:getWidth()*scale
          obj.high = obj.img:getHeight()*scale
      end
        end
        fsupdated = 0
    end
end
```

If the fsupdated variable is 1, this function now your game.scaler function to recalculate a new scale for each card relative to the size of the screen.

Additionally, the function cycles through each of the hand, horde, back, and grab decks and applies the new size to the cards in play.

Finally, it sets the fsupdated to 0 so that no further size updates are triggered until the user changes the screen settings again.

Launch the game and change the screen setting now. Take note of what scales properly and what does not. Spend some time thinking about the problems you see, and try to predict what function contains the problem code.

Usability

One point of confusion you might detect after testing is that there's no explicit way to return to the game from the menu screen. On one hand, it's reasonable to expect that since the user had to press Esc to get to the menu screen in the first place, the user can probably guess that pressing Esc again returns to the game. On the other hand, making the user think too hard about an interface can be frustrating, so there's no reason to leave it up to chance.

Add a menu option to return to a game already in progress. Phrases like "Exit menu" and "Resume game" can be taken many different ways: exiting the menu could also mean exiting the application, and resuming a game could mean loading a previously saved game. A good interface uses the clearest possible language, which in this case is simply "Return to game".

First, add the new option to the menu entry array in menu.lua.

```lua
local entries = { "New game", "Load saved",
    "Window mode", "Save", "Return to game", "Quit" }
```

Change the menu maximum value, which is used by the wrap function to move the selection marker from the bottom of the menu back to the top, to match the number of menu entries. Previously, the menmax value was hard coded to 5, but by now you are familiar with some new array shortcuts, so it makes sense to make the menmax a dynamic value that sets itself to whatever number of items in the entry array.

```
local menmax = #entries
```

In the menu.draw function, change the for loop to repeat itself from 1 to whatever value is contained in the menmax variable. The first and last line in this code block are for context.

```
love.graphics.setBackgroundColor(0.1,0.1,0.1) --for context
for i=1,menmax do
    if i == selection then --for context
```

The addition of a new entry has pushed the Quit option back to item 6, so adjust the menu code.

```
elseif selection == 5 then
    game.activate()
elseif selection == 6 then
    love.event.quit()
end
```

Scaling Adjustments

Generally, measurements that need to change dynamically are more predictable when they are based on a single point of authority. All the scaling problems you are witnessing in your test are bugs in the game.draw function, where there is heavy reliance on card.x and card.y values. Since there are several arrays defining cards, the values stored in various card values are unpredictable. There is also some dependence on the pad value, which defines a margin around the edges of the screen, but it changes depending on the screen size. And finally, while the slot variable provides the width of the cards, there's no value at all for the height of cards in relation to the screen size.

In summary, the layout of a dynamically resizable game must be based on the size of its parent window.

To fix your scaling bugs, first determine the aspect ratio (width divided by height) of your cards. This value will help determine the relative height of cards regardless of size. Create a global variable for this value at the top of game.lua.

```
ratio = 1.37
```

Next, change the values for the player's draw deck (the card back). The first and last lines are for context.

```
card = back[1] --for context
love.graphics.draw(glow,pad,HIGH-slot-(slot*ratio),0,scale,
scale,0,0)
love.graphics.draw(card.img,pad,HIGH-(slot*ratio)-pad,0,scale,
scale,0,0)
love.graphics.setColor(0,0,0) --for context
```

Notice that the new method of placing the glow and the deck relies exclusively on values derived from the screen size, and not at all on card-specific variables. As usual in programming, there are actually several different ways to arrive at the same solution, but this is the most efficient; an alternative is to leave the code unchanged, and use screen size calculations to update the important card variables, but that requires updating values in several places, whereas the screen size calculations are made once and then can be used many times. Any time you have the opportunity to require the computer to do less work, you are *optimizing* your code, and that's always a good thing.

The same principles apply to the AI's deck.

```
card = back[2] --for context
love.graphics.draw(shadow,WIDE-(slot)-pad,slot+(slot/4),0,scale,
scale,0,0)
love.graphics.draw(card.img,WIDE-pad,slot+pad+slot/4,0,-1*scale,
-1*scale,0,0)
```

The running score for the player's hand also needs an update.

```
love.graphics.printf(tostring(handval),(slot)-slot/2,HIGH-
(slot*ratio)-pad-pad,slot/2,'center')
```

And for the running score for the AI.

```
love.graphics.printf(tostring(hordeval),WIDE-(slot/2)-pad*2,
(slot*ratio)+pad,slot/2,'center')
```

The screen text announcing the winner and loser requires the same adjustment, because the screen size ratio is not necessarily the same between its windowed mode and its fullscreen mode (depending on the resolution the user's physical monitor is). Still in the game.draw function, update the printf statements to match this code block.

```
if progress < 2 then
    love.graphics.printf("Level " .. level,0,HIGH-(slot*ratio)-
    (pad*ratio)-72,WIDE,'center')
end

if winner == "hand" then
    lastwon = 1
    love.graphics.printf("You have won!",0,(slot*ratio)+
    (pad*ratio)-72,WIDE,'center')
elseif winner == "horde" then
    lastwon = 0
    love.graphics.printf("You have
    lost.",0,(slot*ratio)+(pad*ratio)-72,WIDE,'center')
```

```
elseif winner == "tie" then
    lastwon = 0
    love.graphics.printf("Tied
game.",0,(slot*ratio)+(pad*ratio)-72,WIDE,'center')
end
```

The 72 in each line is the font size of the onscreen text. By now,
you're hopefully suspicious of *any* hard coded value, so you're probably
wondering whether even this value ought to become relative. In fact, you
could make the font size more dynamic by either using some calculation to
determine the optimal size depending on screen size, or you could create
an array of font sizes for specific ranges of screen sizes. As screen sizes vary
wildly in sizes, from mobile phones to 4k monitors, this is a worthwhile
exercise, but one left for you to manage on your own.

All of these changes have affected the grab code. When a player selects
a card, it's added to the grab array, but it's also moved up the screen and
given a particle effect, very precisely placed just under its top border.

In this case, changing the values of one or two or even three grabbed
cards is manageable, so for each card in the grab array, adjust the Y
position and then use that value to calculate the position of the particle
effect. Since all values are relative to the screen size, the particle effect is
anchored to the card size even when the card size has changed to fit a new
screen size. Find and update this code block in your game.draw function.

```
for i,obj in pairs(grab) do --for context
    local count = 1            --for context
    while count < obj.wide/mana:getWidth() do --for context
        obj.y=HIGH-(slot*ratio)-pad*2
        love.graphics.draw(parti,obj.x+(mana:getWidth()*count+1),
        obj.y+32/2)
        count = count+1 --for context
    end                     --for context
end -- for context
```

Notice that the particle effect line uses 32/2 instead of the old pad/3 calculation to position the particle image below the card's top border. This is dependent on the particle image, so if you have changed or plan on changing the particle seed image, you must adjust the value 32 to match the height of your custom image. To make this kind of change even easier, you could create a variable at the top of the file to define the height of the particle image, and then use that variable in this code. That way, all the values you need to change are easily found at the very top of your file, saving you from having to search through your code for all the hard coded values requiring updates. Again, this exercise is left to you to do on your own time.

When the player's hand is drawn, you must change the code so that items in the grab table are moved up to their new Y position, and items in the hand table stay in position.

```
for i,obj in pairs(hand) do --for context
    if game.isselected(obj,grab) then
        love.graphics.draw(obj.img,obj.x,obj.y,0,scale,
        scale,0,0)
    else
    obj.x = pad+(slot*i)
    obj.y = HIGH-(slot*ratio)-pad
    love.graphics.draw(obj.img,obj.x,obj.y,obj.r,scale,
    scale,0,0)
    end
end --for context
```

Try playing the game again to experience dynamic switching of screen sizes. Make adjustments and changes as required, and remember to commit your changes to Git once satisfied.

Save States

Save states for games are a nice convenience for users, and generally expected in modern gaming. Luckily, there's a wide range in what users accept for save states. Some games save every last detail of a game so that when you resume a saved game, it's as if you had only paused the game. Others save less information, placing you back at a waypoint or checkpoint. Still others only save your level and nothing else.

Considering that Battlejack falls within the puzzle or card game genre, saving just the player's level would probably be acceptable by most users. However, Lua's heavy use of tables makes saving and restoring complex data easy, so Battlejack can have full save state support.

There are two bundles of information that need to be saved: there's the player information and the game state. Player information is anything that remains true regardless of a game round, such as whether or not the game is in fullscreen mode, and what level the player has reached. Game information is anything specific to the current round, such as the contents of the draw decks and the player's hands.

You will use two different methods of saving this information, and the information is saved to two separate locations on the user's drive. Player information is generally referred to as the user *configuration* and the game information is *game data* or just *data*.

Create a new file called saver.lua in your project directory. Open it and add a package.path and a requirement of the inifile module. Also, establish a table to hold the functions you will create for it.

```
package.path = package.path .. ';local/share/lua/5.3/?.lua'
inifile = require('inifile')
saver = {}
```

One of the most common errors when saving and loading data in an application's code are missing files or directories. For instance, if you write Lua code to save a the file bar.conf in a directory called foo, if Lua can't find the foo directory, then Lua crashes.

Lua has no way of knowing whether a file or a directory exists, so you must write a function for this. This is a low level operation that is usually the domain of the operating system, and as such Lua's os function has some tools that can help solve this puzzle. Lua functions are documented on the Lua website (www.lua.org/manual) and also in the book *Programming in Lua* by Roberto Ierusalimschy (Lua.org, 2016), the official Lua guide from the language creators.

While there is no function to determine whether a file or directory exists, the os.rename function requires that a file or directory *exists* in order to successfully rename it. It's a little bit of a hack, but by invoking os.rename on a file path, you can parse its output to determine whether it was able to find a file or not.

For example, here's what a successful os.rename action looks like.

```
$ touch foo
$ lua
> os.rename("foo","bar")
true
```

An unsuccessful os.rename action:

```
> os.rename("foo","baz")
nil No such file or directory    2
```

And finally, here is an edge case in which os.rename finds a file but is unable to rename it.

```
> os.rename("foo","bar")
nil Permission denied    13
```

By assigning each part of the output to a variable, you can determine whether or not a file path exists. Add this code to your saver.lua.

```
function saver.exists(path)
    local success, err, num = os.rename(path, path)
    if not success and num == 13 then
        return true
    end
    --returns true or false
    return success
end
```

User Configuration

To save user configuration, you must create a global table in game.lua called conf, and establish a default location for where the configuration file is to be saved. Add the last line from this code block.

```
grab  = {} --for context
up    = {} --for context
earn  = {} --for context
conf  = {} --user config
```

This default location is not arbitrary. In the computer world, everyone benefits from standards. Standards are conventions that programmers mutually agree to follow in order to ensure compatibility. Most modern low-level computing standards are defined by the open source POSIX specification, while user-level specifications for Linux are defined by freedesktop.org. Operating systems that are not open source often follow a combination of open standards and their own standards. You have the option of following one or the other, but since the open standards are available to all, this book follows those.

Freedesktop.org defines two hidden directories in a user's home for configuration and application data. The .config directory contains configuration data and .local/share contains application-specific data files.

Enter these new variables near the top of the game.lua file.

```
home = os.getenv('HOME')          --for context
d    = package.config:sub(1,1) --for context
confdir = home .. d .. '.config' .. d .. 'battlejack' .. d
datadir = home .. d .. '.local'  .. d .. 'share' .. d
```

Use these variables to build a table containing user configuration options, and write those options to the drive in a new userdata function in saver.lua.

```
function saver.userdata()
    conf.user = {}
    conf.user.level = tostring(level)
    conf.user.fullscreen,fstype = love.window.getFullscreen()

    -- does config directory exist?
    if not saver.exists(confdir) then
        os.execute("mkdir " .. confdir)
    end

    inifile.save( confdir .. d .. 'battlejack.ini', conf, "io" )
end
```

The if statement that invokes saver.exists is a subroutine that ensures the destination for the save file exists. If it does not exist, the os. execute function runs the mkdir command on the operating system to create the directory. The mkdir command works on Linux, MacOS, BSD, and Windows.

The last line of the code block uses the inifile library to save the conf table to a file. It uses the io Lua module to create the file.

Now modify menu.lua so that it uses your new saver library. Place the requirement at the top of the file.

```
require("saver")
```

When you originally created the menu, you used a placeholder for selection 4. Erase it and put in a call to the function you have just created.

```
elseif selection == 4 then
    saver.userdata()
```

Game Data

Saving the game data is theoretically a simple matter of taking all the tables that contain game information and dumping their contents into a file. That's a lot of code to write, and also potentially prone to error if a table is very complex. It's also a common task, however, so a user on the lua-users. org website created a handy script to save and load tables. This is the sort of script you might usually find with Luarocks, but it just happens that this script has never been entered into the Luarocks repository, so it just exists on the Internet.

Download the script from lua-users.org/wiki/SaveTableToFile or from the code included with this book. However you obtain it, save it in your project directory, in the local/share/lua/5.3/ folder, as table_save.lua.

Caution   You must rename the file from its default table.save-- 1.0.lua to table_save.lua to avoid Lua from interpreting the file name as a table.

The functions from `table_save.lua` are going to be used by both `saver.lua` and `game.lua`, since the former needs to save table to files and the latter needs to load those files back into tables. To keep with the convention of keeping global variables all in one place, add `table_save.lua` as a requirement for `game.lua` (the functions will be available to `saver.lua` because the functions become part of the application's global namespace).

```
require("card")
require("msg")
require("table_save")
```

In `saver.lua`, create a new function to process the game data, and make sure the appropriate directory structure exists, using the variable for your `datadir` you created in `game.lua`.

```
function saver.gamedata()
    if not saver.exists(datadir .. 'battlejack') then
        os.execute("mkdir " .. datadir .. 'battlejack')
    end
```

Next, add the code to save the card decks to files. The syntax of the save function provided by `table_save.lua` are given in comments at the top of the file.

```
table.save( table , filename )
on failure: returns an error msg
```

Of course, if you only provide a filename, Lua would do exactly as it is told and save the files into your current directory, so you must interpret `filename` broadly to mean the *path* to the file you want to create.

Add this to the `saver.gamedata` function.

```
--current hand
table.save(hand,datadir .. 'battlejack' .. d .. 'hand.tbl')
--current horde
table.save(horde,datadir .. 'battlejack' .. d .. 'horde.tbl')

--current masterdecks
table.save(deck,datadir .. 'battlejack' .. d .. 'deck.tbl')
table.save(ai,datadir .. 'battlejack' .. d .. 'ai.tbl')
end
```

Launch the game and start a round. Once you have drawn one or two cards, go to the menu screen. Save the game and then quit.

In a terminal, view the user config file that has been created.

```
$ ls ~/.config/battlejack
battlejack.ini
# cat ~/.config/battlejack/battlejack.ini
[user]
level=0
fullscreen=false
```

Confirm that the decks have also been created.

```
$ ls ~/.local/share/battlejack/
ai.tbl  deck.tbl  hand.tbl  horde.tbl
```

Loading a Save File

The inverse of saving a game is loading a game. This is a little more complex than the save process, because there is so much setup when starting a new game, which is "clobbered" by loading in existing data. Because loading a game replaces the game.new and game.setup functions when invoked, the loading process happens in the game.lua file.

First of all, you want to ensure that you're facing a clean workspace when loading a saved game. Currently, the slate is cleaned by game.new, but if you move the cleanup code to its own function, then you can use it again in your loading code.

Take these lines from game.new and place them into a new function called game.cleanup.

```
function game.cleanup()
    collectgarbage()
    game.blast(deck)
    game.blast(ai)
    game.blast(hand)
    game.blast(horde)
    game.blast(back)
    game.blast(grab)
    winner   = nil
    progress = 0
    game.scaler(WIDE,790)
end
```

Call the game.cleanup function at the top of the game.new function.

```
function game.new()
    game.cleanup()
```

Create a new function called game.load for loading in user and game data. Call the game.cleanup function at the top, and load the user configuration in using the inifile library.

```
function game.load()
    game.cleanup()
    if saver.exists( confdir .. 'battlejack.ini' ) then
        local userconf = inifile.parse( confdir .. 'battlejack.
        ini', "io" )
        level = userconf['user']['level']
```

```
else
    print("no user INI found")
end
```

The next logical step would seem to be loading the game data, but first there's another bit of code that usually only happens in game.new: generating a background.

Any time you can, you generally should reuse code. Move the following lines of code from the game.new function into a new game.background function.

```
function game.background()
    ground = love.graphics.newQuad(0,0,WIDE,HIGH,150,150)
    tile   = love.graphics.newImage('img' .. d .. 'tile.jpg')
    tile:setWrap('repeat','repeat')
end
```

Similarly, the draw decks (the card backs) are generated in the game. setup function. You can't call game.setup because it clobbers several settings that game.load performs, such as building the decks, shuffling the decks, adding a Joker card, and so on. Move this code from game.setup into a new function called game.backs.

```
function game.backs()
    -- create GUI decks
    -- hand back
    card = Card.init("c","v","back",pad,HIGH-(slot*ratio)-pad)
    --HIGH-slot-(pad*2))
    back[#back+1] = card

    -- horde back
    card = Card.init("c","v","back",WIDE-(slot/2)-pad,slot-(pad))
    back[#back+1] = card
end
```

Call the function at the top of game.setup.

```
function game.setup()
    game.backs()
    deck = game.setsplit("card",1,deck,2) --for context
```

Call both of your new functions in your game.load routine:

```
    else --for context
        print("no user INI found") --context
    end --for context

    game.background()
    game.backs()
```

Loading tables back into Lua is explained in the comments at the top of the table_save.lua file.

```
table.load( filename or stringtable )
```

```
Loads a table that has been saved via the table.save function
```

```
on success: returns a previously saved table
on failure: returns as second argument an error msg
```

The tricky thing about Battlejack's tables are that some contain card *descriptions* and others contain cards saved as tables. Luckily, you have a card building library that converts card descriptions to drawable cards, so reconstructing hand and horde is a trivial for loop. Enter this code at the bottom of your game.load function.

```
    game.background() --for context
    game.backs()      --for context

    --get deck states
    if saver.exists( datadir .. d .. 'battlejack' .. d .. 'hand.
    tbl' ) then
```

```
  tbl = table.load( datadir .. d .. 'battlejack' .. d ..
  'hand.tbl' )
end

--build decks
for i,obj in pairs(tbl) do
  card = Card.init(obj['color'],obj['value'],obj['face'],
  obj['x'],obj['y'])
  hand[#hand+1] = card
end

if saver.exists( datadir .. d .. 'battlejack' .. d ..
'horde.tbl' ) then
  tbl = table.load( datadir .. d .. 'battlejack' .. d ..
  'horde.tbl' )
end

for i,obj in pairs(tbl) do
  card = Card.init(obj['color'],obj['value'],obj['face'],
  obj['x'],obj['y'])
  horde[#horde+1] = card
end

  --get deck states
if saver.exists( datadir .. d .. 'battlejack' .. d .. 'deck.
tbl' ) then
  deck = table.load( datadir .. d .. 'battlejack' .. d ..
  'deck.tbl' )
end
if saver.exists( datadir .. d .. 'battlejack' .. d .. 'ai.
tbl' ) then
  ai = table.load( datadir .. d .. 'battlejack' .. d ..
  'ai.tbl' )
end
```

```
    game.activate()
end
```

Once the load process is finished, it calls `game.activate` to put the user back in the game.

Launch the game and load your saved game. Try this process a few times, and play through a few games. Take note of any errors or glitches you encounter.

Homework

The next chapter makes no further changes to the game code aside from adding sounds to the experience. That means the game is basically feature-complete, so any glitches or unoptimized code you find are permanent unless you change it.

Here are some examples, but don't limit yourself to this list.

- Only one save is supported. Program a method to permit different save slots.

- If a user forgets to save their game before quitting, they lose their progress. Devise a system to avoid this.

- The text of the message screen isn't always positioned correctly for all screen sized. Change the code of `msg.lua` to fix this problem.

Remember to commit your changes to Git to preserve snapshots of your progress.

CHAPTER 11

Sound

Real video games have sound effects. Everyone knows that. So if you deliver a game to someone without sound, they immediately notice that it's missing the audio. This chapter introduces the most important love. audio functions and integrates sound into Battlejack.

Finding Audio

As with any game asset, the first problem with adding sound effects to your game is that you need sound effects. Of course, open culture on the Internet has a few potential solutions, and so does your Raspberry Pi, if you're up for some manual labor.

Before continuing, create a folder in your project directory for your sounds. To save on typing, name the directory snd.

```
$ cd ~/battlejack
$ mkdir snd
```

The website freesound.org is a treasure trove of sound effects. Search for terms like *level up*, *power up*, *ambient music*, *game*, and so on, to rummage through thousands of professional sound effects that are free to use. The licensing of each sound can differ, so look at the requirements set by the creator; some require attribution, some forbid using their work in commercial products, and others require nothing.

© Seth Kenlon 2019
S. Kenlon, *Developing Games on the Raspberry Pi*,
https://doi.org/10.1007/978-1-4842-4170-7_11

There are other websites loaded with sounds, but you don't have to limit yourself to reusing other people's work. You can create your own high-quality sounds on your Raspberry Pi with Linux Multimedia Studio, better known as LMMS.

LMMS

LMMS is a music production suite available for free on your Raspberry Pi. Whether or not you call yourself a musician, LMMS makes it easy to lay down a beat, synthesize new sounds, sample, loop, distort, enhance, and mix. LMMS comes with ready-to-use instruments, presets, and samples, making it one of the easiest music applications on any platform to get started on.

Install LMMS as usual.

```
$ sudo dnf install lmms
```

It takes a while for the full package to install, since there are so many synths and effects bundled with it, so be patient. Once installed, launch LMMS from the application menu.

Whatever you make in LMMS ends up in the Song Editor window. This is where you *sequence*, or schedule, sounds. If you are using LMMS to create sound effects, then everything you sequence should happen immediately in the left-most block. If you are using LMMS to make background music for your game, then the sounds happen gradually, over several blocks from left to right.

By default, the Song editor (see Figure 11-1) has four channels (triple oscillator, sample track, beat/bassline, automation) already populated, but these are only example tracks. As you create sounds, you add your own.

Figure 11-1. *The Song Editor window*

On the far left of the LMMS window are vertical tabs. When clicked, each tab opens a panel. Click the star icon tab for a Presets panel (see Figure 11-2) containing sounds and synthesizers that you can use to create your sound effects and music bed. More can be found in the musical note tab.

Click and hold some of the sounds to get a feel for what's available.

Figure 11-2. *LMMS preset panel*

Building a Sound Effect

Once you find a sound that you like, drag the sound into the left panel of the Song editor. This creates a new track in the Song editor, which is the one that you work in to create your sound effect.

This example uses Presets ➤ ZynAddSubFX ➤ Fantasy ➤ 0037-ImpossibleDream5.xlz.

In the Song editor, double-click the first black square in the ImpossibleDream5 track. This opens the Piano Roll editor (see Figure 11-3). As the name implies, this is the digital equivalent to the rolls used in old-fashioned player pianos. Notes are entered into the matrix of the roll so that they are triggered automatically as your song plays.

Since you're only designing a sound effect, keep your "song" (such as it is) under 2 or 3 seconds. This example creates a sound effect for messages announcing that new cards have been added to the player's deck, so the mood is happy and empowering.

Figure 11-3. *Piano Roll (or matrix) editor*

The important buttons in the Piano Roll editor are the pencil and the eraser. The pencil enters new notes into the matrix, while the eraser removes them. You can hear (but not enter) notes by pressing the keys of the keyboard along the left side of the window.

If you're unfamiliar with making music, don't be afraid to experiment. Discover the wonders of a well-constructed arpeggio, or the raw thrill of a power chord. There's no wrong way to design sound effects. If something sounds good to you, then use it.

When you're happy with your first sound effect, go to the File menu and select Export.

In the Export window (see Figure 11-4), navigate to the snd folder in your project directory. At the bottom of the Export window, set Files of type to Compressed OGG-File (*.ogg). This format is common in the game industry because it is an open source format that renders a very small file size, meaning your sound files don't result in an impossibly large game package once you're ready to distribute. Name the file powerup.ogg and click Save.

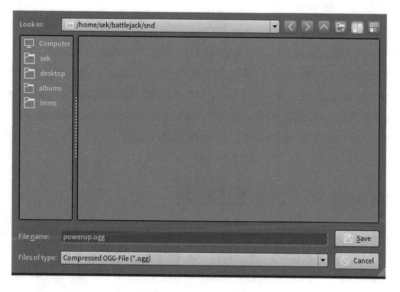

Figure 11-4. Export window

In the Export project window that appears, keep the default settings and click the Start button.

Repeat this process for each sound effect that you want to create. So that you only have one LMMS file per project, you can use the same Song editor for each sound effect. Just mute the tracks that you're finished with as you go. The Mute button for each track is the green light on the left end of the Song Editor track label, as in shown in Figure 11-5.

Figure 11-5. *Muting a track*

As you work, be sure to save your LMMS project. By default, you are prompted to save into a lmms folder in your home directory. This is acceptable, since you won't be distributing the LMMS project along with your game. The sound effect exports, however, must always be saved into the snd folder in your Battlejack project directory.

Listening to Your Effects

To hear your sound effects as they will play in your game, navigate to your snd directory on your desktop and click the .ogg file that you want to hear. The default music player, called Sayonara (see Figure 11-6), opens with that file as the sole item in a playlist in the left panel.

Figure 11-6. *Sayonara player*

Adjusting Export Length

Depending on your aesthetic, some sounds that you use may have a long "tail," meaning that they echo for a few seconds after the notes themselves have ended. The synth preset ImpossibleDream5 is an example of such an effect, and if you listen to the file in Sayonara, you can hear that the file ends before the sounds fade.

To fix this, return to LMMS. Mute any of the tracks that you don't need, and unmute the one that you do. Play the track and watch the timer in the top left of the LMMS window while listening for the sound to fade. It doesn't need to fade out completely, especially if you intend to play background music during the game. When the sound is mostly faded, take a mental note of how many seconds have elapsed.

Stop playback and move the playhead in the Song editor to the position, in seconds, when the sound faded. With a sound clip using ImpossibleDream5 notes that last about 2.5 seconds, you might position the playhead at 10 seconds.

Finally, click the black grid boxes between the sound clip and the playhead (see Figure 11-7). This marks those squares as occupied with sound, even though there are no notes being played.

Figure 11-7. *Creating a buffer at the end of a track*

Export the track again and play it in Sayonara for quality assurance.

Creating Music

Making music for your game is basically the same process as making sound effects, only longer. There's plenty of Creative Commons and royalty-free music online, so you don't have to compose your own game music. However, creating your own music for your game can be fun and rewarding.

Since Battlejack is just a battle card game, the music doesn't need to be much more than a background soundscape, without too much activity or complexity to distract the player from the actual game. In fact, regardless of what kind of game you are composing for, the music you use must be capable of looping, since you can never predict just how long it will be needed.

Unlike most simple sound effects, music composition will probably require more than one track in your Song editor. The sample code included with this book includes two LMMS project files so that you can see how tracks and sound clips in a song fit together.

When you're ready to export your music, use the same settings as you did for your sound effects, with one exception. In the Export project window (see Figure 11-8), select "Export as loop (remove end silence)" so that your music can be looped in LÖVE.

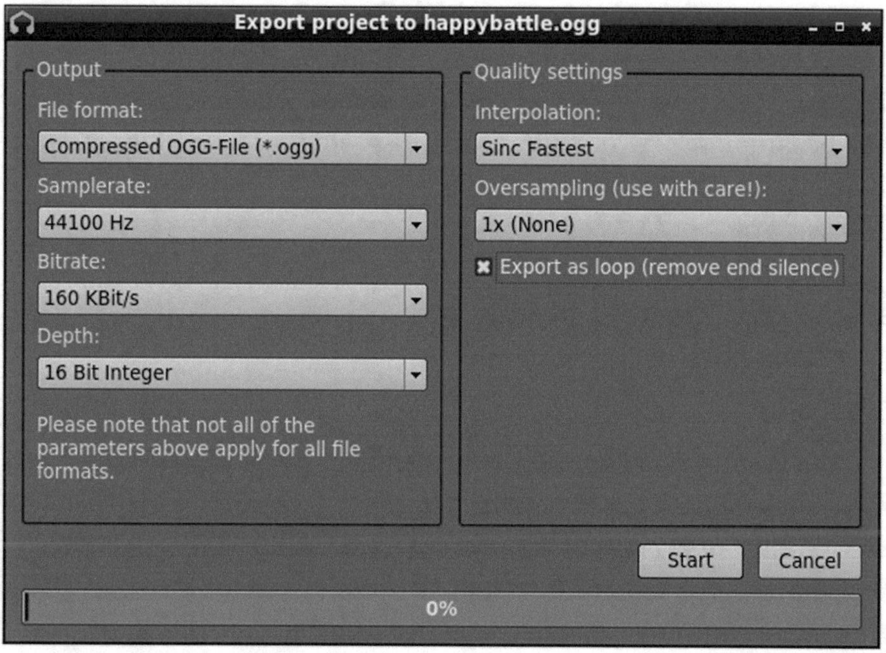

Figure 11-8. *Exporting*

LMMS can't guarantee that your music will loop seamlessly; designing seamless loop points is an art all its own, but you can experiment with ways to disguise loops that don't work, or you can just incorporate a fade-out and fade-in so that the loop, while noticeable, is at least innocuous.

Sound Code

To add sounds to your game, you must create a variable for each sound file that you want to play, classifying it as either a *static file* for sound effects or a *stream* for background music. You use this variable to trigger the sound as needed.

For instance, for the powerup message alert, first create a variable at the top of the game.lua file.

```
fxp = love.audio.newSource("snd" .. d .. "powerup.ogg", "static")

function game.load() --for context
game.cleanup()     --for context
```

Trigger the sound when the message screen loads to announce a new powerup. Add this code to the msg.activate function of msg.lua:

```
if earncard ~= nil then
   love.audio.play(fxp)
else -- only one card to display
   return true
end
```

The if statement establishes whether the message screen is displayed to announce a powerup or because a black card was drawn. If a black card was drawn, nothing is done for now, but if a powerup has been earned, then the powerup sound effect plays. Of course, if you have a sound effect for a traitor card, then you can trigger that sound in the else clause.

Background music is established in main.lua. It's up to you whether you create separate music for the menu screen and the game, but in this example, the same music plays behind the music and the game.

Since the music is both instantiated and played immediately, everything happens in the love.load function of main.lua.

```
music = love.audio.newSource("snd" .. d .. "darkbattle.ogg",
"stream")
music:setLooping(true)
love.audio.play(music)
```

For sound files greater than a few seconds, set the file type to stream so that the entire file isn't loaded into memory.

Since the background music is meant to loop, the variable is also set to loop with the :setLooping(true) LÖVE function.

Go through the code of your game and add background music and sound effects for important events.

If you try to play your game, you may notice that all of your audio is badly distorted. This is a known issue and is easy to fix. You will fix it in the next section.

Fixing the Raspberry Pi Sound Settings

LÖVE uses a technology called OpenAL to play sound. OpenAL is a powerful audio driver providing head-related transfer function (HRTF), more commonly known as *3D audio*. For this reason, it's very popular for gaming. As you know, the Raspberry Pi is a low-powered computer, and not exactly known as a "gaming rig." So when you attempt to play high-powered, specialized OpenAL audio through a mini-computer designed for everyday computer tasks, you experience distortion.

> **Note**   This audio issue is specific to OpenAL on a Raspberry Pi
> or other low-powered computers. If you're using something more
> powerful than a Pi, then you do not need to complete this section
> unless you're experiencing distorted audio in LÖVE.

OpenAL can be configured to be gentler with its host system. By default, global configuration files on Linux are stored in the directory /etc (no one's quite sure any more what that stands for, but there's some evidence that it does indeed mean et cetera, which is an oddly imprecise name for such an important folder). Since this directory exists outside of your home directory, it's only accessible by the root user, which you invoke with the sudo command. Edit the OpenAL configuration file using the sudo command to open it in Geany.

```
$ sudo geany /etc/openal/alsoft.conf
```

You must change two lines in the file. First, you need to edit the number of audio frames that occur between audio mixing updates. This is something that usually OpenAL determines on its own, but in the Raspberry Pi, OpenAL is overly optimistic about what its host system is capable of achieving. Find this line:

```
#period_size = 1024
```

The hash (#) character means this line is "commented out," meaning that OpenAL is currently ignoring the line entirely. Delete the hash character (or as programmers usually say, "uncomment"). Change the number of frames in each update period to 2048. The line should now match this:

```
period_size = 2048
```

Next, find this line:

```
#periods = 0
```

This line is also commented out, so uncomment it by deleting the hash character. A low number here (it is explained in the comments of the configuration file) means faster response from the computer when playing sounds. That's the *ideal* but obviously the Raspberry Pi isn't up to the challenge, so set this value to 8. This tells OpenAL to mix audio in advance so that they're prepared for playback when needed, rather than trying to mix all the audio on demand.

```
periods = 8
```

Save the file and close Geany.

Try playing the game now and you will find that all of your audio problems are solved.

Since this is a known issue that you have now solved, create a README file in your project directory, documenting the problem and its solution in the event that you distribute the game to other Pi users.

```
# Audio issues

If you experience audio distortion when playing
this game, edit /etc/openal/alsoft.conf and set these
values.

period_size = 2048
periods = 8
```

This is good practice, since you can't possibly predict what platform any given user will use to play your game.

Homework

Many games provide some control over sound settings. You could add sound options to your menu screen, such as the following.

- Allow the background music to be silenced, leaving only sound effects.

- Allow all sound in the game to be muted.

CHAPTER 12

Roguelike Dungeon Crawler

Dice games and card games are time-honored time wasters, but you probably want to make other kinds of games, too. No book can possibly cover all the different game styles, and how to code them, but by learning dice and cards so thoroughly, you have learned everything you need to generate the mechanics for any genre.

In this chapter, you learn to apply the principles of game design from earlier chapters to a roguelike game.

What's Roguelike?

The exact definition of *roguelike* is the topic of much debate within gamer culture, but generally it's characterized as an exploration game, often set in a top-down dungeon or tomb in a fantasy setting. It emphasizes tactics, with combat being the central mechanic. There's no story, and randomly generated levels and monster encounters are usually revealed little by little as the player progresses through the map. Furthermore, death is permanent, a frustrating tradition mitigated by the fact that there's no win condition, and the next game will be completely different anyway.

© Seth Kenlon 2019
S. Kenlon, *Developing Games on the Raspberry Pi*,
https://doi.org/10.1007/978-1-4842-4170-7_12

The classic roguelike is Nethack, a very old game that uses ASCII characters to represent the hero, monsters, items, and the map itself (see Figure 12-1). More recent examples include Pokemon Mystery Dungeon, Pixel Dungeon, Diablo, Darkest Dungeon, and Runestone Keeper.

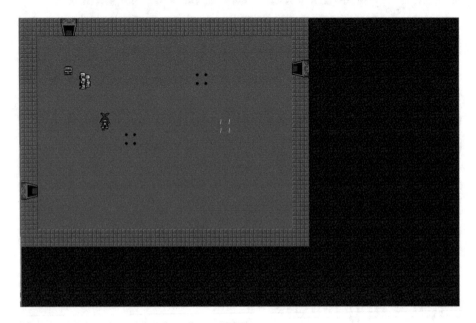

Figure 12-1. *An old-school roguelike*

The roguelike genre is useful because it demonstrates how to translate the same mechanics from dice and card games into a character-driven video game. This chapter emphasizes how to translate what you have learned so far into a game that, on the surface, bears no resemblance to the example games you have created up to this point. There are fewer explanations of the Lua syntax than examples of how all the code you already know is capable of being used in ways that are new to you.

It Looks Good on Paper

As with Battlejack, the smartest thing you can do before writing any code at all is to interpret the game you want to make into a tangible system you can test. As it happens, dynamically generated dungeons for tabletop games have existed for years in the form of random tables. If you've never seen or used a random table, it's worth looking at any Dungeons & Dragons (D&) Dungeon Master Guide as a study of game design. In the context of randomness, Dungeon Master Guides provide tables of various attributes for items that a player might find in an imaginary dungeon while playing this popular tabletop RPG. If a player finds an item, the Dungeon Master may roll dice and then refer to the table to mutually discover, along with the adventurer, what exactly it was that they found. For instance, a die roll of 11 on Table 98 means that the player has found a pair of Bracers of Defense, while a roll of 16 means the player has found Gauntlets of Ogre Power.

The same principle can be applied to the layout of the dungeon itself. For a paper-based example, visit. The system is simple: roll a 12-sided die (d12) for the subjective size of a room, then a d12 again for the general shape of the room, and then a d4 to discover the number of exits that exist in the room.

It's easy to translate this into a digital Lua-based system, and it is easily extended to include all aspects of the game world; the number of monsters in a room, the amount of treasure, the presence of discarded weapons or shields or other gear, and so on.

Most elements of this game can be abstracted out of main.lua into their own tables. Start with the most basic element of a dungeon crawl: the rooms.

Assets

If you're going to build dungeons, you need raw material. Either create or download a few basic elements as tiles, like you did for the tabletop texture of Battlejack. The perspective must be top-down ("bird's-eye). For this game, you need the following.

- Dungeon floor
- Dungeon walls
- Hero
- Two types of monsters
- Two types of traps
- Treasure
- A fireball or similar projectile

The source code for this example game includes the Underworld tile set by Poikilos and Redshrike on OpenGameArt.org, a 32×32–pixel tile set laid out in spritesheets. You can use this set or you can make your own, but this example assumes that your sprites are in spritesheets rather than individual image files, because spritesheets are very common and you should know how to use them.

Once you have your assets in your project's img directory, open a new file called main.lua and set up the basics framework for your code.

```
require("room")
require("door")
require("hero")
require("chest")
require("trap")
require("monster")
require("floor")
require("bolt")
```

```lua
WIDE,HIGH = 960,720
love.window.setTitle(' Ultradimensional Permadungeon ')
love.window.setMode( WIDE, HIGH )

d     = package.config:sub(1,1) -- path separator
t     = 32 -- tile size

hist  = {} --previous rooms, map not implemented
card  = {'n','e','s','w'}
doors = {} --all doors in a room
chests   = {} --all treasure chests in a room
traps    = {} --all traps in a room
monsters = {} --all monsters in a room
bolts    = {} --magic missiles

local fsize = t+4      --font size
local progress = 0     --steps before a door is hot
local permadeath = 0 --is player dead yet

math.randomseed(os.time())

function love.load()
    -- underworld_load CC-BY-3.0 by poikilos
    -- based on these Redshrike's overworld sprites:
    -- door, quad swirl, basis for wall & creatures
    -- Stephen Challener (Redshrike)
    -- hosted by OpenGameArt.org)
    sheet = love.graphics.newImage("img" .. d .. "underworld_
    load-atlas-32x32.png")
    skull = love.graphics.newImage("img" .. d .. "underworld_
    load-sprites-flameskull-32x32.png")
end
```

As you can tell from the `requires` list, you will create a custom library
for each major element of your dungeon. This code also creates a table
to store similar elements together, defines the tile size as specified by the
spritesheet artist, and starts a random seed.

In the `love.load` function, two new variables are created. The `sheet`
variable contains the main spritesheet, and `skull` contains the object that
will serve as a projectile weapon (yes, the hero of this game throws magical
flaming skulls at monsters).

So far, this is the same process you used to create the table texture in
Battlejack.

Treasure

The simplest library in this game is the treasure chest library, called `chest.`
`lua`. This game uses the simplified mechanic of combining health points
and wealth points, meaning that the more treasure the player finds, the
longer the player lives.

```
Chest = { }

function Chest.init(w,h)
    local self = setmetatable({}, Chest)

    self.x = math.random(t*2,(w*t)-(t*2))
    self.y = math.random(t*2,(h*t)-(t*2))
    self.xp = math.random(10,100)
    self.full = true --set to false when player gets treasure

    --treasure images
    self.state = {}
    --closed by default
```

```lua
self.state[1] = love.graphics.newQuad(6*t,2*t,t,t,sheet:getD
imensions())
--opened
self.state[2] = love.graphics.newQuad(8*t,2*t,t,t,sheet:getD
imensions())

self.img = self.state[1]
return self
end
```

Images are each defined with the newQuad function. Each one extracts some portion of the sheet image. The syntax specifies the X and Y position of the image you want to "cut out" from the spritesheet. Since the spritesheet is laid out in columns and rows, all you have to do is count, starting at 0, and then multiply the result by the tile size. Since this is programming, you're better off letting the computer do the multiplication for you, so the X and Y positions are defined with small equations, such as 6*t and 2*t.

The size of each image is always the same, so t,t is used to set the width and height of the sprite. Finally, sheet:getDimensions() is called to set the source and size of the image that the quad is using as its source.

Traps

Next, create a trap class in a file called trap.lua and add the following code to it.

```lua
Trap = { }

function Trap.init(w,h)
    local self = setmetatable({}, Trap)

    self.x = math.random(t*2,(w*t)-(t*2))
    self.y = math.random(t*2,(h*t)-(t*2))
```

```
self.state = {}
--crack
self.state[1] = love.graphics.newQuad(6*t,15*t,t,t,sheet:
getDimensions())
--pit
self.state[3] = love.graphics.newQuad(11*t,14*t,t,t,sheet:
getDimensions())
--spike trap
self.state[2] = love.graphics.newQuad(6*t,13*t,t,t,sheet:
getDimensions())
--spikesprung
self.state[4] = love.graphics.newQuad(8*t,13*t,t,t,sheet:
getDimensions())

self.sel = math.random(1,2)
self.img  = self.state[self.sel]
self.live = true

-- damage
if self.sel == 1 then
    self.dmg = math.random(1,3)
else
    self.dmg = math.random(3,6)
end

return self
end
```

This library generates a trap object located somewhere within a room
of a given size (specified by the w and h arguments). There are two different
traps, each with two states: there's a crack in the floor that opens into a pit,
and pinholes from which spikes spring. For ease of selection, the image

for the first type of trap is stored in `self.state[1]` and the second in
`self.state[3]`. This way, the virtual die only has to choose between
two numbers, which can be directly applied to which image is used for its
un-sprung state.

Monsters

Create a file called `monster.lua` and open it in Geany. Monsters are similar
to traps. They are placed randomly within the room (defined by w and h
arguments), as is their type. Unlike traps, they have natural armor, which
determines how many bolts the hero must hit it with to kill it.

```
Monster = { }

function Monster.init(w,h)
    local self = setmetatable({}, Monster)
    self.x = math.random(t*3,(w*t)-(t*2))
    self.y = math.random(t*3,(h*t)-(t*2))

    self.face = {}
    self.dmg = 1

    -- armour strength
    if math.random(1,20)%2 == 0 then -- fungus
        self.ac = math.random(5,10)
        self.name = "fungus"
        self.face[1] = love.graphics.newQuad(0*t,0*t,t,t,sheet:
        getDimensions()) --fungus up
        self.face[2] = love.graphics.newQuad(1*t,0*t,t,t,sheet:
        getDimensions()) --fungus up
        self.face[3] = love.graphics.newQuad(2*t,0*t,t,t,sheet:
        getDimensions()) --fungus up
```

```lua
      self.face[4] = love.graphics.newQuad(0*t,2*t,t,t,sheet:
      getDimensions()) --fungus down
      self.face[5] = love.graphics.newQuad(1*t,2*t,t,t,sheet:
      getDimensions()) --fungus down
      self.face[6] = love.graphics.newQuad(2*t,2*t,t,t,sheet:
      getDimensions()) --fungus down
   else
      self.ac = math.random(10,20)
      self.name = "golem"
      self.face[1] = love.graphics.newQuad(9*t,5*t,t,t,sheet:
      getDimensions())
      self.face[2] = love.graphics.newQuad(10*t,5*t,t,t,sheet:
      getDimensions())
      self.face[3] = love.graphics.newQuad(11*t,5*t,t,t,sheet:
      getDimensions())
      self.face[4] = love.graphics.newQuad(9*t,7*t,t,t,sheet:
      getDimensions())
      self.face[5] = love.graphics.newQuad(10*t,7*t,t,t,sheet:
      getDimensions())
      self.face[6] = love.graphics.newQuad(11*t,7*t,t,t,sheet:
      getDimensions())
   end

   -- damage
   if self.face == "fungus" then --fungus
      self.dmg = math.random(6,18)
   else --golem
      self.dmg = math.random(8,24)
   end

   -- xp value for battle
   self.xp = self.ac*3
```

```lua
    self.go = 1 --or 4
    self.img = self.face[1]
    self.battle = false --is it engaged in battle
    self.alive = true

    return self
end
```

Setting images for the monsters is similar to setting images for traps, except that there are many more states for each monster. On this spritesheet, there are at least three images of each monster walking east, and at least three more of each monster walking west. This is significant, because in the animation cycles for the monster, the grouping of images for each monster matters: starting at self.face[1] has the monster facing one way, and starting at self.face[3] has the monster face the opposite direction.

Hero

Create a file called hero.lua and open it in Geany. The code for the hero is as simple as the treasure or trap libraries, although it may look more complex at first.

```lua
Hero = { }

function Hero.init()
    local self = setmetatable({}, Hero)

    self.ani = {}
    for i=0,2,1 do
        self.ani[#self.ani+1] = love.graphics.newQuad((10+i)*t,
        3*t,t,t,sheet:getDimensions()) --right 123
        self.face = "e"
    end
```

```
for i=0,2,1 do
    self.ani[#self.ani+1] = love.graphics.newQuad((10+i)*t,
    1*t,t,t,sheet:getDimensions()) --left 456
    self.face = "w"
end
for i=0,2,1 do
    self.ani[#self.ani+1] = love.graphics.newQuad((10+i)*t,
    2*t,t,t,sheet:getDimensions()) --down 789
    self.face = "s"
end
for i=0,2,1 do
    self.ani[#self.ani+1] = love.graphics.newQuad((10+i)*t,
    0*t,t,t,sheet:getDimensions()) --up 10-12
    self.face = "n"
end

self.img = self.ani[7]
self.x    = t
self.y    = t
self.speed = t/2
--self.hp   = math.random( 8,20 ) --health
self.xp   = 10 --experience .. and health
return self
end
```

This code is lazy, in a good way. There are a total of 12 states for the hero's image: a three-frame walk cycle for each cardinal direction. Instead of typing out all 12 quad definitions, a for loop is used for each direction. Additionally, a variable called self.face is set to make it easy to find out which direction the hero is facing. This is an important variable to determine whether the hero is passing by a doorway or actually passing through a door, and also for determining which way a magic missile (or a flaming skull, as the case may be) is fired.

The self.speed variable defines how quickly the hero moves each turn. The self.xp variable grants the hero 10 points of XP. Other variables, such as self.x and self.y, are created as placeholders, since they will be overwritten almost immediately, when the hero is placed in the room.

Bolt

Create a file called bolt.lua and open it in Geany.

```
Bolt = { }

function Bolt.init(x,y)
    local self = setmetatable({}, Bolt)
    self.ani = {}

    self.ani[1] = love.graphics.newQuad(0*t,0*t,t,t,skull:getDim
    ensions())
    self.ani[2] = love.graphics.newQuad(0*t,1*t,t,t,skull:getDim
    ensions())
    self.ani[3] = love.graphics.newQuad(0*t,2*t,t,t,skull:getDim
    ensions())
    self.ani[4] = love.graphics.newQuad(0*t,3*t,t,t,skull:getDim
    ensions())
    self.img = self.ani[1]
    self.x = x
    self.y = y
    -- direction of fire
    self.face = hero.face
    self.speed = t/2 -- pixels per step
    return self
end
```

This library creates a table for the bolt's images from the spritesheet skull. It sets an initial origin point of self.x and self.y, both of which are defined by the x and y arguments when the bolt is created. Since the bolt is meant to originate from the hero's magical hands, the origin point will always be the same as the hero's current position.

Floor Tiles

The last library you need isn't really a library or class in any traditional sense. It is kept separate from main.lua, because in theory it's easy to swap out with something different. The floor.lua file defines all of the images used to draw the dungeon itself. Everything from floor tiles, wall tiles, doors, dead space, and anything else you want to use when drawing a room.

```
Floor = { }

function Floor.init()
    local self = setmetatable({}, Floor)

    -- floor
    self[1] = love.graphics.newQuad(3*t,10*t,t,t,sheet:
    getDimensions())
    -- wall
    self[2] = love.graphics.newQuad(15*t,10*t,t,t,sheet:
    getDimensions())
    -- door
    self[3] = love.graphics.newQuad(10*t,14*t,t,t,sheet:
    getDimensions())
    -- forbidden zone
    self[4] = love.graphics.newQuad(13*t,6*t,t,t,sheet:
    getDimensions()) -- space
    self[5] = love.graphics.newQuad(3*t,9*t,t,t,sheet:
    getDimensions())   -- lava
```

```
   -- passageway
   self[6] = love.graphics.newQuad(0*t,14*t,t,t,sheet:
   getDimensions())
   return self
end
```

Room

In your project directory, create a new file called room.lua. Design an init function that creates a room of a random size, with a random number of traps, treasure, and monsters in side of it.

```
Room = { }

function Room.init(w,h)
   local self = setmetatable({}, Room)

   -- room dimensions
   self.w = math.random( 4,24 );
   self.h = math.random( 4,14 );

   -- how much treasure
   -- how many monsters
   -- how many traps
   if self.w < 7 or self.h < 7 then
      self.treasure = math.random(0,1)
      self.monster = math.random(0,1)
      self.trap = math.random(0,1)
   else
      self.treasure = math.random(0,2)
      self.monster = math.random(0,2)
      self.trap = math.random(0,2)
      end
```

```
    self.phlogiston = floor[4] --texture for space outside dungeon
    return self
end
```

All decisions about the room and its contents are made with the digital equivalent of rolling a die. The room size is based on the assumption that this game works on a tiled setup, so the room width, for instance, will never be less than 4 tiles nor larger than 24 tiles.

This library isn't finished yet, because it lacks doors. Doors are significant enough, however, to deserve their own class. However, the existence of a door in any given wall is determined by the room itself, so add some code to decide which wall has a door.

```
    self.phlogiston = floor[4] --for context

    -- number of doors
    self.north = bool(math.random(1,20)%2) --row
    self.east = bool(math.random(1,20)%2) --col
    self.south = bool(math.random(1,20)%2) --row
    self.west = bool(math.random(1,20)%2) --col

    return self --for context
end               --for context
```

This code plays a little with probability. Instead of having the computer decide between 0 and 1 for whether or not a door is in a wall, it "rolls" a 20-sided die (d20) and then divides the result by 2, returning the modulo (the "remainder"). The result is the same: either a 0 or a 1, but the probability is a little better distributed.

To transform the 0 and 1 result to a Lua-friendly Boolean value, a custom function is used. The bool function returns false *unless* a value is 1.

Add the following function to room.lua.

```
    return self --for context
end               --for context
```

```lua
function bool(value)
    return ( value == 1 and true or false )
end
```

Finally, it's important to know which door the hero stepped through in the previous room so that the hero can be drawn at the opposite door in the next room. Create a hot table in main.lua to track this information.

```lua
local permadeath = 0 -- is player dead yet
hot = {}
hot['x'] = nil
hot['y'] = nil
hot['name'] = nil

math.randomseed(os.time()) --for context
```

This reveals a problem with randomness, though. Normally, if a hero goes through a door in the east wall, then the hero should emerge in the next room from the west wall. But if the next room has been randomly generated, there may not be a door on the west wall. To fix this, open the room.lua file and create an override for the randomness of door existence. If a door is marked hot, then force a door to exist on its opposite wall.

```lua
    -- if a door is marked hot then
    -- there must be a door in the next room
    if string.sub(hot['name'], 1, 1) == 'n' then
        self.south = true
        self.north = true
    elseif string.sub(hot['name'], 1, 1) == 's' then
        self.north = true
        self.south = true
    elseif string.sub(hot['name'], 1, 1) == 'e' then
        self.east = true
        self.west = true
```

```
    else
        self.east = true
        self.west = true
    end

    self.phlogiston = floor[4] --for context
```

Doors

Your room library decides whether or not a door exists in a given wall, but it doesn't determine a door's physical position. Create a door.lua file and add the following code to it.

```
Door = { }

function Door.init(face,w,h)
    local self = setmetatable({}, Door)

    self.face = face

    if self.face == "n" then
        self.x = (math.random(t,w*t)-t)
        self.y = t
    elseif self.face == "e" then
        self.x = (w*t+(t/2))-t
        self.y = (math.random(t,h*t)-t)
    elseif self.face == "s" then
        self.x = (math.random(t,w*t)-t)
        self.y = (h*t)-t
    else
        self.x = (0+(t/2))+t
        self.y = (math.random(t,h*t)-t)
    end
```

```
    self.go = true
    return self
end
```

The location of each door is determined from a random range from tile 1 (not 0, since a door in a corner would be inaccessible) to the maximum length of a wall (minus 1 tile, to avoid a door in the corner). The door is marked active with the self.go variable, and a field called self.face is created to track which direction the door is facing.

Rogue Code

The code for main.lua is only about 400 lines of code. Most of it is code similar to what you have already done for the previous games in this book, but there are a few new tricks specific to character-driven games for you to learn.

Open main.lua and finish up the love.load function. Create a floor variable containing all tiles from the dungeon, create a font variable and set the drawing color to white, and create a music variable for background ambiance. Finally, create the hero using your hero.lua library, and then call a nonexistent love.first function to place the hero in the first room of a nonexistent dungeon.

```
floor = Floor.init() -- images for room tiles

font = love.graphics.setNewFont("font/pixlashed-15.otf",fsize)
love.graphics.setColor(1,1,1) -- values 0 to 1
hero = Hero.init()
```

```
    music = love.audio.newSource("snd" .. d .. "happybattle.ogg",
    "stream")
    music:setLooping(true)
    love.audio.play(music)
    love.first()
end --for context
```

The love.first function is arbitrarily named. You can call it anything,
such as love.start or love.begin. The point is, you need some function
to serve as the starting point for a new dungeon. The first entrance into
the dungeon is unique from entering any other room in the dungeon
because there is no "hot" door; that is, the hero hasn't left one room to
enter another, so the game must generate a random starting position for
the player.

```
function love.first()
    if hot['name'] == nil then
        hot['name'] = card[math.random(1,4)]
    end
    room = Room.init() --create the room
    love.door() --create the doors

    if hot['x'] == nil then
        print("You enter a dark dungeon.")
        -- set where hero is entering
        if hot['name'] == "n" then
      hot['x'] = doors['n'].x
      hot['y'] = doors['n'].y
        elseif hot['name'] == "e" then
      hot['x'] = doors['e'].x
      hot['y'] = doors['e'].y
        elseif hot['name'] == "w" then
      hot['x'] = doors['w'].x
```

```
    hot['y'] = doors['w'].y
      else
    hot['x'] = doors['s'].x
    hot['y'] = doors['s'].y
      end
      hero.x = hot['x']    --place hero at hot door
      hero.y = hot['y']    --place hero at hot door
      hist[#hist+1] = room   --add room to history stack
    end
    love.treasure() --place treasure
    love.monster()  --place monsters
    love.trap()     --place traps
end
```

You can probably understand this code, even though you've never done anything like this for your other games. The global hot table is analyzed. If the hot['name'] field is found to be nil, then a value is randomly generated from the contents of the card (as in *cardinal* directions) table. A corresponding X and Y value is assigned to hot table, the hero is placed at whatever door has been designated as the hot door, and then functions are called to place treasure, monsters, and traps.

In previous games, you mostly used automatic indexing with your tables. That is, when you created a table, the key you used to get a value from it was always a number. For example, open a terminal and launch an interactive Lua session.

```
$ lua
> hand = {}
> hand[#hand+1] = "red,wizard,1"
> hand[#hand+1] = "red,fighter,7"
> hand[#hand+1] = "red,goddess,9"
```

Given such a table, you can reference values with numbers as the key.

```
> print(hand[1])
red,wizard,1
> print(hand[3])
red,goddess,9
```

A different convention is used for this dungeon game, though. For some tables, custom keys are defined, allowing you to reference data with strings. Try this:

```
> card = {}
> card['color'] = "red"
> card['type'] = "fighter"
> card['value'] = 7
> print(card['type'])
fighter
```

Obviously each convention is useful for different reasons. Since the doors table contains *other tables* (each one called door), you can access information inside each table using the standard dot notation, as in doors['n'].x or doors['e'].y. It's a lot of data to manage, and it can get overwhelming to try to keep track of which table contains data and which table contains more tables, and what data *those* tables contain. When in doubt, iterate through a table and print the values. If you see more tables, then you know that you either need to iterate through another level of tables, or else call table fields directly. There are more examples of both later in this game, so look at them with this in mind.

Doors, for instance, are the means by which a player progresses through the game. You *could* just arbitrarily throw them into a table, but to make it easy to identify each door object, you can give each one created a custom key. Add this function to your code:

```lua
function love.door()
    if room.north then
        door = Door.init("n",room.w,room.h)
        doors['n'] = door
    end
    if room.east then
        door = Door.init("e",room.w,room.h)
        doors['e'] = door
    end
    if room.south then
        door = Door.init("s",room.w,room.h)
        doors['s'] = door
    end
    if room.west then
        door = Door.init("w",room.w,room.h)
        doors['w'] = door
    end
end
```

This function looks at the room table to discover whether a door at a certain position is meant to exist. If it is, then a door is generated with your door.lua class, and placed into the doors table with a key identifying its position as n, e, s, or w.

Monsters and treasures and traps are less important than doors, because it doesn't matter where they are in the room. Create some functions to reference the room table, find out how many of the objects (treasure chest, monster, or trap) are meant to be in the room, and then generate that number of objects.

```
function love.treasure()
    for i=0,room.treasure,1 do
        local j = Chest.init(room.w,room.h)
        chests[#chests+1] = j
    end
end

function love.monster()
    for i=0,room.monster,1 do
        local j = Monster.init(room.w,room.h)
        monsters[#monsters+1] = j
    end
end

function love.trap()
    for i=0,room.trap,1 do
        local j = Trap.init(room.w,room.h)
        traps[#traps+1] = j
    end
end
```

The next job is similar to what you have already done so far, except that it covers entrances into all other rooms that are not the first room. In other words, the love.first function will only ever be called *once* per game: the first room generated. After that, the love.entrance function generates new rooms, monsters, and so on.

```
function love.blast(tgt)
    local count = #tgt
    for i=0, count do tgt[i]=nil end
end
```

```
function love.entrance()
   love.blast(chests)
   love.blast(bolts)
   love.blast(monsters)
   love.blast(traps)
   progress = 0

   room = Room.init()
   love.treasure()
   love.monster()
   love.trap()
   love.door()

   --[[ ACTIVE DOOR ]]--
   if hot['name'] == 'n' then
      hero.x = doors['s'].x
      hero.y = doors['s'].y
   elseif hot['name'] == 's' then
      hero.x = doors['n'].x
      hero.y = doors['n'].y
   elseif hot['name'] == 'e' then
      hero.x = doors['w'].x
      hero.y = doors['w'].y
   else
      hero.x = doors['e'].x
      hero.y = doors['e'].y
   end
   hist[#hist+1] = room --add room to history stack
end
```

You might remember the blast function from Battlejack. It clears out the old data from tables. It's used here because rooms are disposable; once a player leaves a room, they can never return to it. This is a design decision made exclusively to keep the code simple (and it's why there is a hist table tracking each room as they are created, but never actually used for any mechanic).

Draw Function

The draw function is, of course, the place where all the graphics really happen. You already know the basics of this function, so read the code once for comprehension, and then add it to your main.lua file.

First, create a background to fill the game window in places where there is not a dungeon.

```
function love.background(room)
    for c=0, WIDE, 1 do      -- for each column of the window
        for r=0, HIGH, 1 do -- for each row of the window
        love.graphics.draw(sheet,room.phlogiston,t*c,t*r)
        end
    end
end
```

Placing doors on walls is a dangerous prospect, because if they are inaccessible then the room looks poorly coded. To protect yourself from accidentally having doors in corners, create a trim function that forcefully forbids any value greater than or equal to the length of a wall or less than 1 tile.

```
function trim(room,n)
    if n >= room.w*t then
        n=n-t
    elseif n < t then
        n=n+t+t
    end
    return n
end
```

And then draw the room by filling in any outer edge with a wall tile, and any area that is *not* the outer edge with a floor tile. If a door is meant to exist on the wall, draw a door.

```lua
function love.draw()
  --[[ WORLD ]]--
  love.graphics.setColor(1,1,1)
  love.background(room)

  for c=0, room.w, 1 do    -- for each column in room
    for r=0, room.h, 1 do -- for each row in room
    if c == 0 then -- west wall
       love.graphics.draw(sheet,floor[2],t*c,t*r)
       if room.west then love.graphics.draw(sheet,floor[3],
       doors['w'].x-t,trim(room,doors['w'].y),math.rad(-90),1,
       1,t/2,t/2) end
    elseif c == room.w then -- east wall
       love.graphics.draw(sheet,floor[2],t*c,t*r)
       if room.east then love.graphics.draw(sheet,floor[3],
       doors['e'].x+t,trim(room,doors['e'].y),math.rad(90),1,
       1,t/2,t/2) end
    else -- middle ground
       love.graphics.draw(sheet,floor[1],t*c,t*r)
    end -- if i

    if r == 0 then -- north wall
       love.graphics.draw(sheet,floor[2],t*c,t*r)
       if room.north then love.graphics.draw(sheet,floor[3],
       trim(room,doors['n'].x),doors['n'].y-t) end
    end -- if j
```

```
   if r == room.h then -- south wall
      love.graphics.draw(sheet,floor[2],t*c,t*r)
      if room.south then love.graphics.draw(sheet,floor[3],
      trim(room,doors['s'].x),doors['s'].y+t,0,1,-1,0,t) end
   end -- if j
    end --for j
 end --for i
```

The rest of the love.draw function is pretty routine. Draw the traps, treasures, monsters, update the player about their score or death, draw any bolts that have been fired, and then draw the player.

```
--[[ TRAPS ]]--
for k,v in pairs(traps) do
   love.graphics.draw(sheet,v.img,v.x,v.y)
end

--[[ TREASURE ]]--
for k,v in pairs(chests) do
   love.graphics.draw(sheet,v.img,v.x,v.y)
end

--[[ MONSTERS ]]--
for k,v in pairs(monsters) do
   love.graphics.draw(sheet,v.img,v.x,v.y)
end

--[[ STATS ]]--
if permadeath == 0 then
   love.graphics.printf("XP " .. hero.xp,t*2,HIGH-fsize,
   WIDE,'left')
else
   love.graphics.printf("You have experienced PERMADEATH.",
   hero.x,hero.y,WIDE,'left')
end
```

```
--[[ BOLTS ]]--
for k,v in pairs(bolts) do
    love.graphics.draw(skull,v.img,v.x,v.y)
end

--[[ CHARACTER ]]--
love.graphics.draw(sheet,hero.img,hero.x,hero.y)
end --draw
```

Keypressed

Permadungeon is a turn-based game, meaning that the hero moves and then the monsters move. For that reason, player movement happens on each key press, and monster movement happens on each key release.

For movement to happen, the player and monster sprites must be updated to proceed to their next animation frame. Since there are only 3 or 4 animation frames, depending on the object being animated, you need frame counters that can be cycled constantly as the game progresses. Create these at the top of the main.lua file along with your other local variables.

```
bolts  = {}   --for context
local frame = 1      --turn-based frame
local aframe = 1     --animated frame
local fsize = t+4    --for context
```

Another counter is the progress variable. This is a convenience counter that ensures a player is a few steps from the door through which they entered before the game starts looking for doorway collisions; otherwise, the player might accidentally step back through a door as soon as they enter a room. The progress counter is reset each time a room is created.

Here is the player movement block of the love.keypressed function.

```
function love.keypressed(key)
    frame = frame+1

    progress = progress+1

    if frame >= 3 then
        frame = 1
    end

    if hero.x < (room.w*t)-t and
        key == "right" or key == "d" then
        hero.x = hero.x+hero.speed
        hero.img = hero.ani[frame]
        hero.face = "e"
    elseif hero.x > t and
        key == "left" or key == "a" then
        hero.x = hero.x-hero.speed
        hero.img = hero.ani[3+frame]
        hero.face = "w"
    elseif hero.y > t and
        key == "up" or key == "w" then
        hero.y = hero.y-hero.speed
        hero.img = hero.ani[9+frame]
        hero.face = "n"
    elseif hero.y < (room.h*t)-t and
        key == "down" or key == "a" then
        hero.y = hero.y+hero.speed
        hero.img = hero.ani[6+frame]
        hero.face = "s"
    end
```

The next block of code checks for collisions. For that to happen, steal a simplified version of the `collide` function from Battlejack.

```
function collide(x1,y1,x2,y2)
    return x1 < x2+t and
       x2 < x1+t and
       y1 < y2+t and
       y2 < y1+t
end
```

When a collision is detected, things happen. Sometimes, damage is dealt or XP is rewarded. Trap images change to show that the trap has been sprung, and treasure chest images change to the opened state. Combat is kept simple; if the player collides with a monster, the hero takes damage.

```
--[[ TREASURE ]]--
for k,v in pairs(chests) do
    if collide(hero.x,hero.y,v['x'],v['y']) and v.full then
    hero.xp = hero.xp+v.xp --take gold
    v.img = v.state[2]      --close
    v.full = false          --mark empty
      end
end

--[[ TRAPS ]]--
for k,v in pairs(traps) do
    if collide(hero.x,hero.y,v['x'],v['y']) and v.live then
    hero.xp = hero.xp-v.dmg  --take damage
    v.img = v.state[v.sel+2] --change image
    v.dmg = 1                --disarm
    v.live = false           --mark not live
      end
end
```

```
--[[ start BATTLE ]]--
for k,v in pairs(monsters) do
    if collide(hero.x,hero.y,v['x'],v['y']) and v.alive then
   hero.xp = hero.xp-v.dmg --take damage
   v.battle = true
    end
end
```

Door detection is more complex. It only starts when the hero is at least 2 key presses into the room, which prevents accidentally going back through the same door the player entered through. Similarly, you don't want a player to accidentally fall through a door just by crossing its threshold, so you must reference hero.face to verify that the hero is intentionally walking through the door (because the hero and the door are both facing the same way). When a player *does* willfully pass through a door, you must record what wall the door was on so that the player can emerge from the opposite wall in the next room.

```
if progress > 2 then
for k,v in pairs(doors) do
    if collide(hero.x,hero.y,v.x,v.y) and v.go then
   if hero.face == v.face then
      hot['x'] = v.x
      hot['y'] = v.y
      hot['name'] = tostring(k)
      love.entrance()
        end -- if
      end -- if
end --for
progress = 0
end --if progress
end
```

Monster Movement

In the love.keyreleased function, two important things happen: the monsters move, and any bolts that the hero fires are generated. Placing the fire power trigger in the keyreleased function rather than the keypressed function is a good way to reinforce that your player can't just hold down a button and spray bolts out at their enemy. While LÖVE distinguishes between a key press and a key repeat, not all game engines do, so it's good practice to put fire power where you really mean for it to happen.

Creating a bolt is the same as creating a trap or a treasure or monster, except that it only happens when a specific key is released.

```
function love.keyreleased(key)
   if key == "f" or key == "u" then
      local j = Bolt.init(hero.x,hero.y)
      bolts[#bolts+1] = j
      hero.xp = hero.xp-math.random(0,6)
   end
```

Monster movement is similar to player movement, except that their movement is automated. To keep things simple, the monsters move the length or depth of a room, reversing direction if they get within one or two tiles of a wall. To mix things up a little, some of the monsters move with a variable speed.

```
--[[ MONSTERS ]]--
for k,v in pairs(monsters) do
   if v.name == "fungus" then
   if v.y < t*2 then
      v.go = 0
   elseif v.y > (room.h*t)-(t*2) then
      v.go = 1
   end
```

```
  v.img = v.face[v.go+frame]
  if v.go == 0 then
     v.y = v.y+math.random(0,1)*t
  else
     v.y = v.y-math.random(0,1)*t
  end

   elseif v.name == "golem" then -- ice golems
  if v.x > (room.w*t)-(t*1) then ---(t*1) then
     v.go = 1
  elseif v.x < t*2 then
     v.go = 0
  end

  v.img = v.face[v.go+frame]
  if v.go == 0 then
     v.x = v.x+t --math.random(0,1)*t
  else
     v.x = v.x-t --math.random(0,1)*t
  end
   end
end
```

At the end of the function, check the permadeath variable. If it is greater than 0, then the hero has died. As a quick hack around an abrupt stop, this function increments the permadeath counter and then ends the game once the counter is greater than 2.

```
if permadeath > 0 then
   permadeath = permadeath+1
end
```

```
    if permadeath > 2 then
        os.exit()
    end
end --function
```

Bolts and Updates

The final function to write for the game is the love.update function.
This is a standard LÖVE function. You've used it before to check for win
conditions and to update particle effects. In this game, the update function
is needed for out-of-turn motion, specifically for the bolts fired by the
hero. While it might be a valid mechanical choice to make weapon fire
move within the structure of game turns, it's more common that fire power
moves in real time.

Since the bolt animation happens to have four states on its spritesheet
rather than three, a dedicated frame counter that goes all the way up to
four is used. Bolt movement is basically the same as hero and monster
movement, except that when it reaches the limits of a room, it is removed
from the bolts table. If it hits a monster, it deals damage to the monster
and is removed from the table.

Lastly, the function checks the status of the hero.xp variable. If it's less
than one, then permadeath is activated. This variable, of course, signals the
end of the game.

```
function love.update(dt)
    aframe = aframe+1
    if aframe >= 4 then
        aframe = 1
    end
```

```
for k,v in pairs(bolts) do
   v.img = v.ani[aframe]
   if v.face == "e" then
  v.x = v.x+v.speed
   elseif v.face == "w" then
  v.x = v.x-v.speed
   elseif v.face == "n" then
  v.y = v.y-v.speed
   elseif v.face == "s" then
  v.y = v.y+v.speed
   end

   -- still in room?
   if v.x > (room.w*t)-(t*2) then
 table.remove(bolts,k)
   elseif v.x < t then
      table.remove(bolts,k)
   elseif v.y > (room.h*t)-(t*2) then
 table.remove(bolts,k)
   elseif v.y < t then
      table.remove(bolts,k)
   end

   --hit or miss
   for i,j in pairs(monsters) do
      if collide(v.x,v.y,j['x'],j['y']) and j.alive then
      j.xp = j.xp-math.random(0,6)
      table.remove(bolts,k)
      if j.xp < 1 then
         table.remove(monsters,i)
      end
   end
   end
end
```

```
if hero.xp < 1 then
    permadeath = 1
end
end
```

That's all the code there is for a basic dungeon crawler. Launch it, fix any bugs you find, and make your own improvements.

Homework

To keep the code samples concise, there are many deficiencies in the Permadungeon game. Here are some improvements you could make to the game using the principles you have learned from this and previous exercises.

- The monsters are very passive in this game and they move in predictable patterns. Alter the code for the monsters so that after some number of the hero's steps, the monsters move toward the hero until they swarm and kill the hero.

- The combat system in this game consists only of monsters with collision attacks and a hero with a fire bolt. It could be more challenging if some monsters had ranged attacks, as well.

- A more ambitious change would be to equip the hero with two weapon slots, one for melee attacks and one for ranged attacks. The player should have the freedom to switch weapons at the expense of one turn.

- It's difficult to tell when combat is happening. Invent a system that displays hit values and health points on the hero and the monster when combat occurs.

- Make some treasure chests into traps.

- When a monster dies, make it drop loot or healing potions instead of just disappearing.

- Add sound effects.

- Devise a better end game.

CHAPTER 13

Game Distribution

People used to go to computer stores to buy video games. That tradition is mostly relegated to console gaming now, with most PC game and all mobile game purchases happening online. If you want to get your game into the hands of the gaming public, you need to know how to package it and where to post it.

Packaging

Game packaging, from the perspective of a programmer, has nothing to do with literal packaging and marketing. Packaging, in the coding business, refers to how you gather up all the libraries and assets your game depends on so you can effectively deliver it to the public. LÖVE makes it easy, but as every programmer knows, you never package software only *once*. Inevitably, your users are going to find bugs you never noticed, or request features you never imagined, and you're going to have to release updates. That means packaging your game not once but several times over the course of its life, but since you're a programmer now, you should already be asking how you can automate the process so you never have to do the actual work more than once.

As you know from the dice game early in this book, the simplest possible LÖVE game file is a ZIP file containing a valid `main.lua` file. So to package a LÖVE game, all you need to do is gather all of the game's code files, assets, and libraries, and then compress them into a ZIP file.

© Seth Kenlon 2019
S. Kenlon, *Developing Games on the Raspberry Pi*,
https://doi.org/10.1007/978-1-4842-4170-7_13

Throughout this book, each game has been developed in a unique project directory. Even the external libraries you've installed from Luarocks or the Internet at large were placed in a local folder in your project directory. So that's the first requirement sorted.

One of the most common methods of automating software releases is the make file. Not all software projects use a make file, but most use something like it: a script designed to perform routine tasks to save you from making a stupid mistake while packaging up your game.

Open Geany and create a new file called luamake in your Battlejack project directory.

You might recall the command you used to create a game file for your dice project. Lua can use the same command, thanks to the os.execute function, which runs any command you would normally run from the operating system. Add this line to luamake.

```
os.execute("zip battlejack.love -r *.lua deck.ini font img
local snd")
```

Open a terminal window and run the luamake file.

```
$ cd battlejack
$ lua ./luamake
  adding: card.lua (deflated 54%)
  adding: game.lua (deflated 72%)
  adding: main.lua (deflated 55%)
  ...
$ ls -1
battlejack.love
...
```

The make file works as expected. Scripting this simple command ensures that you never accidentally package your game but forgetting to include the images, or the local libraries, or anything essential to the application.

Versioning

One problem with updating an application is that once you release an update, there are different versions of the same application. The last thing anyone wants is to run an old, buggy version of an application after a fix has been released, so it's smart for you and smart for your users to use a versioning scheme.

There are many versioning schemes out there. Applications that develop rapidly and release often tend to use semantic versioning, as described on semver.org. Applications that only release once a year might just use a major version number, like 5 or the release year. Others use code names, or something entirely unique.

You can choose your own schema, but for simplicity's sake this example uses the date to automatically generate a version. In a terminal, try out the standard Linux date command.

```
$ date +%Y
2019
$ date +%Y-%m
2019-06
$ date +%Y%m%d
20190603
```

The date command syntax uses shorthand to request specific aspects of the current date. The final command in the example output displays the year, month, and date with no delimiter. Normally, a version string is separated with dots, but some file managers on Android have trouble opening .love files that contain any more dots but the final one, so for compatibility, avoid complex version strings for now.

Lua has a similar syntax in its os.date function. Update luamake to match this.

```
d = os.date("%Y%m%d")
```

```
os.execute("zip battlejack-" .. d .. ".love -r *.lua deck.ini
font img local snd")
```

The output of luamake would be, for example, battlejack-20190603.love. That's better than just battlejack.love but it ignores the possibility that you might make two updates to your application in one day. Ideally, you would only actually publish the most recent update, but crazy things happen in software development.

Commands issued directly to the operating system are described by the POSIX standard, and the convention is that the first string you type into a terminal is the command itself, followed by optional options or flags (which are often, appropriately, optional), and then by an argument. For example.

```
$ readlink --canonicalize luamake
/home/pi/battlejack/luamake
```

In this example, readlink is the command, --canonicalize is the option, and luamake is the argument.

Lua is a command, and so it uses the same syntax, which means your luamake file can accept an optional version number chosen by you at run time.

When you run a Lua application, even a simple script like luamake, everything you type into the terminal is recorded by Lua in a table called arg. For example, if you were to type this.

```
$ lua ./luamake --foo bar
```

The arg table for luamake contains luamake in arg[0], --foo in arg[1] and bar in arg[2].

By looking at the arg table in a Lua script, you can get extra parameters from the user (in this case, you).

Add this `if` statement to `luamake` to detect an optional version number.

```
d = os.date("%Y%m%d")

for k,v in ipairs(arg) do
   if v == "-v" or
   v == "--version" then
      ver = arg[k+1]
   end
end

if ver == nil then
   ver = 0
end

os.execute("zip battlejack-" .. d .. "-" .. ver .. ".love -r *.
lua deck.ini font img local snd")
```

Its syntax is now.

```
$ lua ./luamake --version 1
...
$ ls *love
battlejack-20190602-1.love
```

If you provide no version, then it is assumed to be 0, producing a file like battlejack-20190603-0.love.

Help Message

Since your formerly simple one-line script now has an optional flag, you should document how to use it. It might seem obvious now, but you'll thank yourself in a month when you go back to fix a bug and suddenly realize you don't remember how to generate a release package.

Help messages are best when they're intuitive. You shouldn't need a help message to tell you how to get a help message. The traditional flag for help is --help and, for lazy typists, -h. However, you can add other flags if you have other ideas. It's your toolchain, after all. Change the for loop in luamake file to match this.

```
for k,v in ipairs(arg) do
    if v == "-v" or
    v == "--version" then
        ver = arg[k+1]
    end
    if v == "-h" or
    v == "--help" then
        help()
        os.exit()
    end
end
```

There is no help function yet, so add one that explains to your future self how to use your custom luamake command.

```
local function help()
    print("luamake       : generate a .love package")
    print("luamake -v 2 : set the iteration version to 2")
    print("luamake -h   : print this help message")
end
```

Executable

On Linux, you're encouraged to write your own commands. You've just written one, but it doesn't *feel* like a command because you have to use Lua to run your script.

The lua command is what's called a binary executable, meaning that it has been translated from code to a machine language. If you were to open lua in Geany, you wouldn't see code, you'd see garble.

The Lua programs you have been writing are scripts that are interpreted by either LÖVE or Lua directly. Without LÖVE or Lua, your scripts are just plain text files.

You can, however, make your Lua script act like a binary executable file by adding a special line, *shebang* or *magic cookie*, of text at the very top of the file.

```
#!/usr/bin/env lua
```

This defines what application to use to run the text contained in the script.

Not just any file can be launched as if it were an application. Linux won't run the contents of a file unless it is explicitly marked as *executable*. This is done with the chmod command. Make sure you are in your project folder and run this command.

```
$ chmod +x ./luamake
```

Now you can treat luamake as an independent command.

```
$ ./luamake --version 3
```

Distribution

You can distribute your LÖVE games anywhere online. If you have a website, then you can post your game for download and you're officially a game distributor. Posting something online and people knowing that your game exists, however, are two different things.

For better exposure, you can also post your game on established indie game distribution sites.

Online

Open source programming is everywhere, and several very large websites are eager to host your code. Popular code hosting sites include GitLab. com, GitHub.com, NotABug.org, Bitbucket.org, SourceForge.net, and many others. Most are based on Git, which you have been using during the course of this book to track your work.

These hosting services provide not only a no-cost online storage space for your game projects, they also provide the ability to open your code for others to see. Sometimes that means other people will learn from your hard work, and other times it means someone smarter than you will improve your code and teach you something new. It's the open source model, and it's popular for a good reason.

Some of the hosting services even provide basic homepages so you can design a simple page or two to advertise your game's features.

Because GitLab itself is open source and can be installed on private servers, it's become popular among both hobbyists and professional software houses, so its web interface is worth learning. All of them are practically the same, so learning GitLab teaches you the same principles you need to use the others.

Register an account on GitLab.com (you are required to confirm your email address, so use a valid email) and log in.

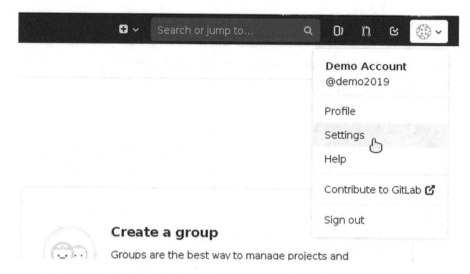

Figure 13-1. *The Settings menu item in Gitlab*

In User Settings Figure 13-1, click the SSH Keys link in the left panel. An SSH key is a pair of files used to authenticate one computer to another. This level of trust isn't necessary when you're just downloading a file from the Internet, but when you *upload* something to someone else's servers, they want to make sure you're always the same person you claim to be.

You must generate an SSH key to authenticate to your remote Git server. Open a terminal and create a new hidden folder in your home directory called .ssh, and then make it private with chmod 600, meaning that only you have access to the folder (do this even if you are the only person using your computer, because SSH requires it as part of its security policy).

```
$ mkdir --parents ~/.ssh
$ chmod 600 ~/.ssh
$ ssh-keygen -t ed25519 -f ~/.ssh/git.key
```

You are prompted for an optional password. This is a password for access to the key itself, in the event that your key should fall into the wrong hands. You don't have to use a password, in which case anyone with your SSH key files would have access to your online Git account.

The result of the command are two files in a hidden directory called `.ssh`.

One file is a private key file, which you must never post anywhere. It's like a password; you would never tell anyone your password, regardless how official they may appear or however nicely they may ask. Treat your private SSH key file the same. Your private SSH key is named `git.key`, because you named it that as part of your command.

The other file created by your command is `git.key.pub`, and it is meant specifically to be distributed *publicly*. If you place your *public* key on a server, then when you try to access that server using your private key, authentication is successful. You can think of these SSH keys as a "friendship necklace", with two interlocking pieces that are relatively meaningless on their own but perfectly complete together. In more technical terms, the public file is like a padlock and the private file is the key that unlocks it.

View your SSH public file by opening it in Geany, or in a terminal with this command.

```
$ cat ~/.ssh/git.key.pub
```

Select the text of your key from `ssh-ed25519` to the very end and select Edit ➤ Copy.

In your web browser, paste your public key text into the Key text field, and then click the "Add key" button Figure 13-2.

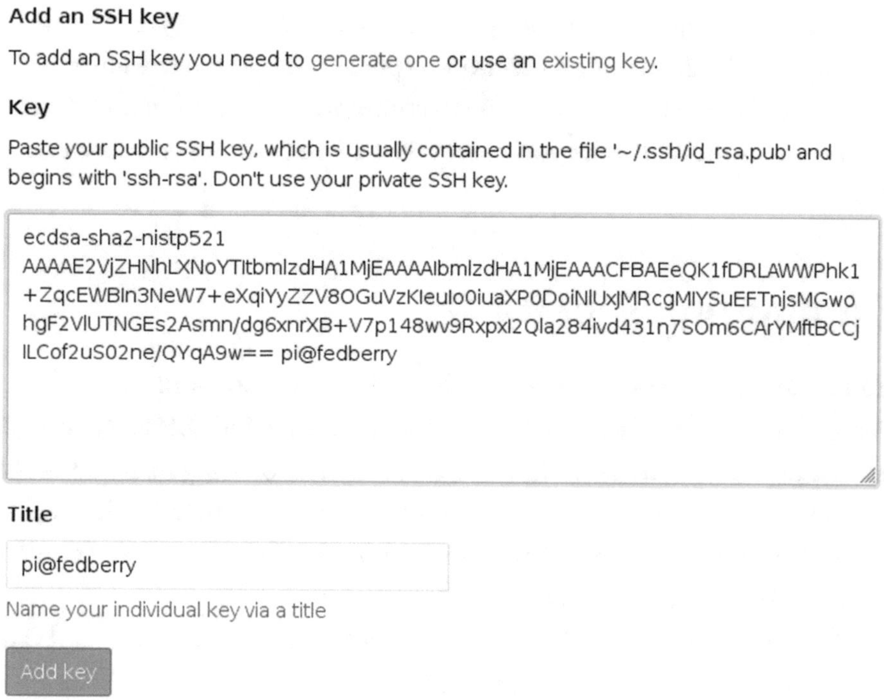

Add an SSH key

To add an SSH key you need to generate one or use an existing key.

Key

Paste your public SSH key, which is usually contained in the file '~/.ssh/id_rsa.pub' and begins with 'ssh-rsa'. Don't use your private SSH key.

```
ecdsa-sha2-nistp521
AAAAE2VjZHNhLXNoYTItbmlzdHA1MjEAAAAIbmlzdHA1MjEAAACFBAEeQK1fDRLAWWPhk1
+ZqcEWBIn3NeW7+eXqiYyZZV8OGuVzKleulo0iuaXP0DoINlUxJMRcgMlYSuEFTnjsMGwo
hgF2VIUTNGEs2Asmn/dg6xnrXB+V7p148wv9Rxpxl2Qla284ivd431n7SOm6CArYMftBCCj
ILCof2uS02ne/QYqA9w== pi@fedberry
```

Title

```
pi@fedberry
```

Name your individual key via a title

`Add key`

Figure 13-2. *Adding an SSH key to Gitlab*

Click the Projects menu in the top left of the GitLab interface and select Your Projects. This takes you back to your GitLab home screen. Since you haven't created any projects yet, click the "Create a project" button.

On the New Project screen, provide a name for your project, such as battlejack. Optionally, you can provide a short description of the project. Set the project visibility, keeping in mind that public code increases your chances of getting useful feedback and also that others will be able to learn from you.

Click the "Create project" button to instantiate the project on GitLab's servers.

After the project is created, you are brought to the project's page, which provides instructions on how to post your code to the empty project. It assumes you know how to configure SSH, however, so there are some additional steps you must take before pushing your code to GitLab.

Configuring SSH for Git

You've configured your SSH keys on both your computer and on the Git server, but the git on your computer doesn't know what SSH key to use (or even that you want to use SSH, since Git is capable of using many different protocols). If you provide the git command or git-cola an SSH address, then Git knows to use your SSH configuration. The problem is, you don't have a SSH configuration yet.

Create a file in the hidden .ssh folder in your home directory, and call it config. You can do this in a terminal.

```
$ touch ~/.ssh/config
```

Open this file in Geany. Since it's a hidden file, it may be easiest to do this from a terminal.

```
$ geany ~/.ssh/config &
```

Enter this configuration into your config file.

```
host gitlab
    hostname gitlab.com
    user git
    identityfile /home/pi/.ssh/git.key
```

The user value *must* be git. That's not your username, but most online Git hosts use git as the generic username for all of their users, since they rely exclusively on SSH keys to actually identify each person.

The value of identityfile, however, may differ on your computer. For instance, this example assumes that your username is pi, which is often the default user on a Raspberry Pi Linux distribution. If you've created your own user, or changed your username, or aren't using a Pi at all, then change pi for your actual username.

If you don't know your username, use the whoami command to find it out.

Save the config file.

Pushing to Git

Now that SSH is fully configured for Git, you can add your remote Git project to your local project directory. This example uses the Battlejack, but this process is the same for any project you work on, as long as you have a local directory that is being tracked by Git and a remote Git server upon which you've created an empty project.

First, go to your project directory on your computer.

```
$ cd ~/battlejack
```

Add your remote Git server to your Git project. The URL you use in your command must include *your* GitLab account name rather than demo2019. Find the Git project location on your GitLab project page, either in the instructions at the bottom of the page or near the top of the page under the project name (make sure you get the SSH version of the URL, not the HTTPS version, since the latter doesn't provide write access).

```
$ git remote add server git@gitlab.com:demo2019/battlejack.git
```

This command does exactly like it reads: Git is adding a *remote* (that is, not in the same location as you) destination called server, with the address of git@gitlab.com:demo2019/battlejack.git. The name server is arbitrary, and exclusively for your own use. It is the shortened term that refers to git@gitlab.com:demo2019/battlejack.git. Some users name it origin, others call it upstream, and so on.

If you prefer to use git-cola, open your project and select File ➤ Edit Remotes. In the Edit Remotes window, click the + button in the lower left corner.

In the git-cola dialogue box that appears, enter server for the name field, and the Git project location, such as git@gitlab.com:demo2019/battlejack.git, for the URL field.

You can now push your code to your remote Git server. In a terminal.

```
$ cd ~/battlejack
$ git push --set-upstream server HEAD
```

This command is very specific; it tells Git to push your code and to set the remote location (called server) as an "upstream" location. That's fancy software development terminology meaning that Git is not only pushing code *to* your server, but also should, in the future, pull changes from it.

In the future, you need only issue this simpler command.

```
$ git push server HEAD
```

If you prefer git-cola, go to the Actions menu and select Push. In the Push window that appears, set Remote, along the top of the window, to server. Select the Set upstream option along the bottom of the window (you only need to do that the first time you push to a project on your server), and then click the Push button.

git-cola warns you that the target server is devoid of any of your code, so a new branch is being created to mirror your local project directory. Click the Create Remote Branch to accept.

Itch.io

Itch is a leading indie game distribution site, offering video games for Linux, Windows, and Mac. Developers can post games and set either a fixed price, no price, or pay-what-you-want. Some games, like Mr. Rescue, are even programmed with LÖVE.

Itch is not curated or moderated. This means that you can post nearly anything to it. There's no approval process. With this freedom comes great responsibility; don't post the games that you've written haven't had anyone else test, don't post half-baked games that are bound to frustrate your users. Post your games after extensive testing and refinement. The Itch audience and your own reputation will thank you.

You can sign up for Itch for free and post your game. Tag your game with relevant information, such as the genre and game engine, to help people find your game, and set it as fully cross-platform, since LÖVE itself runs on Linux, Windows, and Mac.

Lutris

Lutris is not exactly a game distributor, but a game aggregator. For fans of retro, indie, and open source gaming, Lutris is a unified library for thousands of games. Unlike Itch, it is a curated collection, meaning that not just any game gets posted. However, you can write your own Lutris installer and distribute that independently, or you can wait until game is nearly perfect, well-tested, and ready to stand up to the scrutiny of serious gamers, and then post it.

Lutris is something of a hybrid system. Lutris.net is an online community, with a library filled with installer files. It does *not* distribute games, only scripts to make games already downloaded by a user appear in the user's Lutris desktop application.

Lutris, the desktop application, is a game library that makes it easy for a user to browse through their personal collection and launch a game regardless of whether it was written for Linux, Windows, a web browser, LÖVE, and many other platforms.

A Lutris install file is a simple script written in YAML, a popular configuration format. A Lutris installer needs to communicate to Lutris where a game executable is located, and what application on the user's computer must be used to launch it.

Using the Battlejack project as an example, create a file called battlejack.yml in your home directory. Open this file in Geany.

First, you must identify where the game file is located. Assuming your game is freely available online with no purchase required, then you can have the Lutris installer download it for your user.

```
files.
- lovefile: https://example.com/games/battlejack-2018.09.03-3.love
```

Lutris has no storefront, so if you are charging money for your game, then you must prompt the user to point Lutris to the game (the .love file) they have already purchased and downloaded.

```
files.
- lovefile: N/A:Please select the Battlejack.love file.
```

This configuration option tells Lutris that there is one file required for this game, but that the location is not yet known. When a user installs the game, Lutris prompts the user to select the .love file on their hard drive.

Regardless of how the game is acquired, the location of the game file is assigned to a new variable called lovefile.

Next, you must tell Lutris how to run the game. You know the full command to run Battlejack is love battlejack.love, and that's exactly the same command that Lutris must use, although the syntax is specific to the YAML configuration.

```
game.
- args: $GAMEDIR/$lovefile
- exe: love
```

This configuration block tells Lutris that the actual executable command is `love`, and the argument to pass to LÖVE is a variable containing the name of the game directory (which is defined by the user during install) and a variable containing the name of the game file.

Next, the actual install is described in YAML. For LÖVE games, there isn't really an installer; they just play in LÖVE. All your configuration file needs to do is make sure that the `.love` file is placed in whatever directory the user has told Lutris to use as their game folder. This value is `$GAMEDIR`, defined by Lutris.

```
move.
- dst: $GAMEDIR/$lovefile
- src: $lovefile
```

Finally, you must alert Lutris that this game requires LÖVE to run. LÖVE has its own Lutris installer, so should anyone install your game, they have a similar one-click access to LÖVE, as well.

```
requires: love2d
```

Your installer is finished. Log in to lutris.net, add a new game, paste in your installer, and submit it for moderation. While you're at it, add a screenshot of your game, a description, and other data so that people can see that it's a legitimate, playable game.

Mobile Market

The mobile market, including phones and tablets, is a major game outlet, and LÖVE is perfectly suited for creating mobile games. LÖVE is available for both Android and, *technically*, iOS. Android is open source, so it's easier for both users and developers to install LÖVE onto it than onto iOS.

Note   Even the Android version of LÖVE lacks a few important features at the time of this writing, although it's being updated constantly and new features are appearing rapidly.

Apple places restrictions on what users and developers may do on Apple devices. Highly technical users can load LÖVE onto their Apple mobile device, but most will not. Until Apple decides to permit independent app usage and development, iOS is a difficult market for small app developers. However, now that you understand Lua and advanced programming concepts, you can explore Apple-sanctioned app development if that's your primary target.

It is smart, however, to at least *plan* for both, even if you don't guarantee full compatibility with the platform you cannot, for whatever reason, test. The more universal you make your game, the more people are able to play them.

Installing LÖVE on Android

To play a LÖVE game on your Android mobile device, you have to install LÖVE itself. You might find LÖVE in the Google Play store or in F-Droid. org, but it's best to download the latest available version directly from love2d.org.

Android packages are delivered as .apk files. Your mobile device might warn you that such a file is dangerous or harmful, presumably for fear that you are installing malware. It's safe to ignore this particular warning (see Figure 13-3) since you're familiar with the LÖVE project, and download the package.

Figure 13-3. *Installing LÖVE on Android*

Your mobile may offer to install the APK file once it's downloaded. If not, you must install a file manager so you can get to your files. Your mobile probably doesn't have one, or else not a very good one, so download the open source Amaze file manager from https://play. google.com/store/apps/details?id=com.amaze.filemanager.

Once installed, launch Amaze, locate the `.apk` file you downloaded, and tap it to install.

You may be warned again that the APK installer is from an unknown source. It's perfectly safe to ignore this error.

There's no use in launching LÖVE directly once it's installed. It's just the game engine, so what the user actually launches is a `.love` file. The Amaze file manager, and many others, prompts the user to select which application to use.

The game launches, and reads taps as `mousepressed` and `mousereleased` events Figure 13-4.

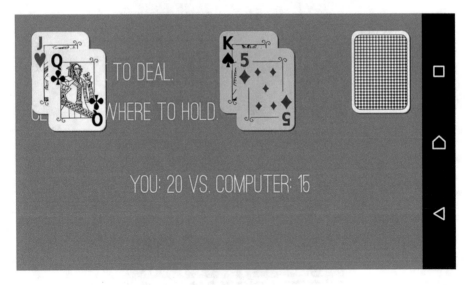

Figure 13-4. *Blackjack on Android*

Limitations of LÖVE on Mobiles

LÖVE on Android and iOS is a rapidly developing technology, so there are fewer and fewer limitations every month. Whatever state the engine is in, however, there are a few things to keep in mind when developing for mobiles.

- There's no expectation that mobile devices have a keyboard, so mousereleased and mousepressed should be favored in a mobile game.

- For menus, define buttons rather than text entries so it's easier for a finger or stylus to trigger a click event.

- Screen sizes on mobile devices vary wildly, and as the popularity of Android continues to grow, so will the range of resolutions. If you want your game to run on palm-sized phones, paper-sized tablets, and big-screen TVs, you must design your game to scale.

- Furthermore, the aspect ratio and pixel density on some mobile devices won't match your computer screen. If what you see on your screen isn't matching what's ending up on your device, try doubling a value or similarly adjusting your game dimensions (or better yet, make your game resolution independent with proper scaling). For example, the spec sheet of a phone with a high pixel density might report that its screen is 300 pixels wide, but your game only fills the screen if you design it with at 600 pixels wide instead.

- At the time of this writing, LÖVE lacks permission to write data to the phone's internal storage. That means you can't get the os.getenv('HOME') location or create save files yet.

Watch love2d.org for updates.

CHAPTER 14

Next Steps

With this book, you have learned the foundations of not just Lua, but of programming. You have access to the building blocks of very advanced code. All you have to do now is use the knowledge you have gained for new projects.

How to Practice

You're familiar with the old saying *practice makes perfect,* and it should be no surprise that it applies as much to programming as to anything else. You cannot hope to become an efficient, comfortable programmer without weeks and weeks, and then months and months, of practice. The key is to find an excuse to use Lua. Make Lua work for you. Make it do stuff that you don't feel like doing yourself. You have already learned how to use Lua to build and release your software, for example, so find other small tasks for Lua to do for you.

Note If you want to create a GUI application in Lua, there are several toolkits you can use. Obviously, there is LÖVE itself, but it is intended as a game engine. For a generic GUI libraries providing common widgets like buttons and text fields, try TekUI at tekui. neoscientists.org, SUIT for LÖVE at github.com/vrld/SUIT, and Luce at github.com/peersuasive/luce.

© Seth Kenlon 2019
S. Kenlon, *Developing Games on the Raspberry Pi,*
https://doi.org/10.1007/978-1-4842-4170-7_14

Sometimes, learning new tricks on computers seems like a waste of time. For instance, you already know how to start a basic LÖVE project, but imagine how much you would learn by creating a Lua script to generate fresh project directories and even basic file starters. Find common, everyday tasks that you find yourself doing frequently, and spend time programming an application or command to help you accomplish them. The task itself may only take you a minute or two to do, and programming a solution might take you a few days, but you'll learn a lot, and after the 300th time of doing the same old task, you'll thank yourself for the application you created. And after your 300th script, you won't even be able to remember when you didn't think like a programmer.

How to Learn

Of course, practice in principle is one thing, but actually generating code that functions is another. Sometimes, you will want to do something in code that you have no experience with, and no reference point for where to begin.

The Lua and LÖVE functions you have learned from this book were relatively easy for you to discover because this book presented them to you and showed you how to use them.

A big part of learning a programming language is learning what functions it has to offer you. Lua functions are documented in full at www. lua.org/manual/5.3, in the Index section. Every function of Lua is listed and documented. For LÖVE, see love2d.org/wiki/love.

The Lua site is highly technical and doesn't provide many examples, so it can be difficult to understand. However, *Programming in Lua* by Roberto Ierusalimschy (Lua.org, 2016), the principle architect of Lua itself, is an excellent resource for both the language and usage of its functions.

How to Read Technical Documentation

Any time you are about to use a new library (like `inifile` or `table_save.lua`) or even a new programming language, you should go to its technical documentation or to the source code itself and read it. You don't necessarily have to read it like a novel, but you should have a passing familiarity with what the library or language provides you so that you know where to start, and you don't spend a day implementing something that a library gives you for free.

As you've probably started to notice from writing them yourself, functions have two parts: input and output. As long as you keep that in mind, you can read technical documentation easily and use any function you dig up.

For example, assume that you are using Lua to program an interface to help users create a password that is at least 15 characters long. You need a way to count the letters in a string (the string `foo` contains three letters, the string `foobar` has six, and so on).

You already know some tricks that count items. For instance, you can find the number of items in a table with the `#table` notation, and you know how to create loops with counters. You could probably spend some time researching this problem and find a reasonable example online on how to implement it. But what you'd also find is that Lua already has a function called `string.len` that solves your problem.

You have never used the `string.len` function, so it might be intimidating to understand how to use it. Here is its online documentation:

```
string.len (s)
Receives a string and returns its length. The empty string ""
has length 0. Embedded zeros are counted, so "a\000bc\000" has
length 5.
```

To read how to use this function, find out those two essential components of every function: input and output. The input to a function is an argument, so (s) is its input. The documentation says that s is a string.

The output of a function is what it *returns*. Sometimes this is a literal return statement in its code, while other times it's variables that get set while the function runs. In this example, the function returns the length of s, so you can expect an integer.

Knowing the required input and expected output, you can guess how to use the string.len function. Since Lua has an interactive mode, you can even test it before adding it to your actual code.

```
$ lua
> print( string.len("foo") )
3
> print( string.len("foobar") )
6
```

Use this learning method with all the technical documentation for Lua, LÖVE, and any other programming library or language that you are using.

Leveraging Open Source

Finally, Lua is open source. It has a worldwide community of users who openly communicate with one another about how the language is used, how common problems are solved, how specific functions work, and much more. If you're not used to the culture of open source, then you're probably not accustomed to this kind of sharing of knowledge. It's a conversation, so join in, be polite and respectful, answer questions when you can, and ask well-researched questions with lots of context and code samples when you need help.

CHAPTER 14   NEXT STEPS

Learning Other Languages

You should spend more time with Lua once you have finished this book, at least until you are comfortable programming in the language. Lua is a simple, efficient, and cohesive language, so there are relatively few functions to learn. It's a manageable language, especially when compared to bigger ones like Python, Ruby, Java, and PHP. That's a feature that you'll come to appreciate after trying more complex languages.

On the other hand, Lua's minimalism renders a sparse language, meaning that you have to create your own functions for things that other languages have as built-in features.

Some languages, like Python and Java, are so widely known that it seems everything is already done for you; all you have to do is download a library, and most of the hard work is done. Of course, this is not true in practice, because every program ends up requiring customization, but the more popular a language, the greater the choice you have between libraries and frameworks.

The good news is that once you're comfortable enough with Lua to sit down and code something from scratch in an afternoon or two (or seven, depending on the size of the project!), you'll find that learning a new language comes easy. Once you internalize the "grammar" of programming, learning the vocabulary is easy, and often something you can do as you code.

The question is: do you need to learn another language?

Learning a second or third programming language can be useful primarily for compatibility. For instance, if you want to write a plugin for an application that only offers plugin support for Python, then it's useful to know Python. If you want to write native applications for Android, then you should learn Java. If you want to get a job at a company that has built its business on Ruby, then you should learn Ruby.

You might hear murmurings that one language isn't good for one task, and that another language is better for other tasks, as if programming languages were built with a specific set of applications in mind. While it's true that sometimes a language is designed in such a way that its available functions happen to favor one type of job or another, strictly speaking, a programming language is just an interface to machine instructions. Don't be confused by the mélange of choice. Learning additional programming languages add to your perspective on code, your toolkit for getting things done efficiently, and your *curriculum vitae* when looking for work.

And learning a new language can be done *with this book*. LÖVE is specific to Lua, but most major languages have game engines. And even if your target language lacks a game engine, you can still use the structure of these lessons to learn. Start with simple programs, like a dice roller, and then try something more ambitious, like a simple card game. Explore arrays and other data constructs. Learn to read data from disk and how to write it back out. Learn to write your own libraries or modules and how to `require` or `include` them. And finally, try a bigger project like Battlejack or Permadungeon to stretch your understanding of the language.

Homework

As this book's final assignment, you are encouraged to sit down with a pen and some paper to design the next game or application you want to create with Lua. Spend some time on it. Design something useful and slightly more ambitious than you think you can manage.

Next, break the application down into learnable components. You haven't learned how to drag and drop GUI elements, for example, and yet you know everything you need to make it work (hint: `mousepressed` combined with a custom `collide` function ought to work). Look at your long-term goals and write small applications that may not even serve a purpose other than to teach you a new trick or two.

Once you have learned all the parts of what you want to build, then it's just a matter of implementing it all in one big code base.

Whether or not you feel like you understand everything there is to understand about Lua, programming, game design, Linux, and software development in general, you *are* a programmer now. So go program something!

APPENDIX A

Drag and Drop

The examples in this book have primarily used clicking or key presses for user interaction. LÖVE is capable of responding to other forms of input, such as gamepads, touch screens, and mouse movement.

All of the input functions are documented on love2d.org/wiki, so mostly you can use them as easily as key presses and mouse clicks. However, dragging and dropping requires more code than simple if statements.

A word of caution: dragging and dropping as the only way to interact with an application has accessibility issues. Selecting a source and a target with either a click or a series of key presses is easier for both users who need a screen-reader or have limited mobility or are just plain uncoordinated, while controlling a mouse can be difficult. Dragging and dropping also assumes that whatever device your application is running on has the ability to process a drag and a drop; while most devices today have either a touch screen or a mouse, you never know what tech will bring in the future.

On the other hand, dragging and dropping is a valid mechanic, and it can be useful for some styles of games.

© Seth Kenlon 2019
S. Kenlon, *Developing Games on the Raspberry Pi*,
https://doi.org/10.1007/978-1-4842-4170-7

Draggable object

For this demo, you need an object that you can drag. In practise, this object would be whatever game asset you want your user to move. For this example, create a file called dot.lua and create the essential attributes: the X and Y coordinates, the item rotation, and whether or not the item is currently moving.

```
Dot = { }

function Dot.init(x,y)
    local self = setmetatable({}, Dot)
    self.img = love.graphics.newImage("img.png")
    self.x = x
    self.y = y
    self.moving = 0 --is it being dragged
    self.r = 0 --rotation
    return self
end
```

Code

The main code doesn't contain anything you haven't already encountered, it just uses concepts in a way that's new to you.

A mouse press uses collision detection to determine whether the user has clicked on a movable object. Even though there's only one movable object in this example, all movable objects are in a table, which this code calls hot. If the object that has been clicked is movable, then it is rotated as a visual cue and its moving variable is set to 1. The love.update function ensures that the X and Y values of any moving object in the hot table are constantly updated.

A mouse release action sets the object's rotation back to its original orientation and sets its moving variable back to 0.

Create a second file called main.lua, and add this code:

```
require("dot")

hot = {}

function love.load()
   Dot = Dot.init(300,300)
   hot[#hot+1] = Dot
end

function love.update(dt)
   for i,obj in ipairs(hot) do
      if obj.moving == 1 then
      --DEBUG print(obj.x,obj.y)
      obj.x,obj.y = love.mouse.getPosition()
      end
   end
end

function love.draw()
   for i,obj in ipairs(hot) do
      love.graphics.draw(obj.img,obj.x,obj.y,obj.r,1,1,79,79)
   end
end

function love.mousepressed(x,y,btn)
   for i,obj in ipairs(hot) do
      if x > obj.x and
      x < obj.x + obj.img:getWidth() and
      y > obj.y and
```

```
      y < obj.y + obj.img:getHeight() then
      obj.moving = 1
      obj.r = 0.3
        end
    end
end

function love.mousereleased(x,y,btn)
    for i,obj in ipairs(hot) do
       obj.moving = 0
       obj.r = 0
    end
end
```

Add any image file, called img.png to your project and test the code. You should be able to drag and drop the object around your game window.

To detect whether one object has been dragged onto another object, add more collision detection to this code to detect whether two objects are overlapping or not. It's the same principle as detecting mouse clicks.

APPENDIX B

Using Git

Git is vital technology in modern software development, so the more comfortable you are with it, the better. Researching Git online can be overwhelming, though, because writing software is a complex industry, and Git can adapt to nearly every development style. Learning Git in this book is useful because it limits the scope of what you need to learn. This appendix covers the Git basics that you need to follow the coding exercises in this book and in your daily computing life.

You can create a Git repository within any directory. While it is technically possible to make your entire home directory one big Git repository, it is not recommended. Logically, a Git repository is best when it has clearly defined boundaries. A Git repository makes the most sense when it encompasses a specific project or set of data. For instance, if you have set up Geany in a specific way, you could manage its configuration folder with Git; that's not what you would traditionally think of as a project, but it has a single, clear purpose and set of data.

To create a Git repository, change the directory to the folder you want to use as the basis of the repo. In this example, the directory is called project. Then issue this command:

```
$ mkdir ~/project
$ cd ~/project
$ git init .
```

© Seth Kenlon 2019
S. Kenlon, *Developing Games on the Raspberry Pi*,
https://doi.org/10.1007/978-1-4842-4170-7

The command is `git`, and the option is `init`. The argument, a single dot, means *here*; in other words, it ensures that Git initiates a repository precisely where you are currently "parked" in your terminal.

A directory is a Git repository if it contains a hidden folder called `.git`.

```
$ ls --almost-all
.git/
```

If you prefer to use git-cola, launch it, and then click the New button in the lower-left corner of the git-cola window. You can either select an existing directory or create a new one, and git-cola instantiates the `.git` directory.

git add

To add a file to a Git repository, use the `git add` command. This command marks a file as a trackable object for Git.

To try this out yourself, you must create a sample file. You can use Geany or another text editor to do this, if you want, but it's also valid to use the `echo` command in the Bash shell. The `echo` command does exactly what you probably imagine: it echoes whatever you type back at you.

```
$ echo "print('hello world')"
print('hello world')
```

However, in a terminal, you can redirect anything the computer prints back at you into a file with two >> symbols. If a file doesn't exist, one is created automatically.

```
$ echo "print('hello world')" >> hello.lua
$ ls
hello.txt
```

Create a second file called dummy.lua. It can contain whatever text you like.

```
$ echo "print('Dummy file')" >> dummy.lua
```

You have just created two files, but Git is not aware of either file because they have not been added to Git.

If you're working with git-cola, select File ➤ Refresh or press Ctrl+R to refresh. Your files appear in the Status panel.

Tell Git to track the hello.lua file.

```
$ git add hello.lua
```

In git-cola, right-click the file in the Status panel and select Staged. The result is shown in Figure B-1.

Figure B-1. *Git add in git-cola*

git commit

Letting Git track a file and actually committing a change made to a file are two different things. Adding a file gives Git permission to manage the file. Committing a file tells Git to record changes made to a file, which in turn lets you play those changes back, or rewind the changes to revert to a previous version, or even fast-forward to changes that don't yet exist (because those changes were made by someone else on your team).

Commit your sample `hello.lua` file now.

```
$ git commit --message "created hello.lua"
```

The `git commit` command doesn't take a specific file as an argument. It commits the current state of your repository, which includes anything you have told Git to track.

In git-cola, add the commit message to the text field in the Commit panel, and then click the Commit button, as shown in Figure B-2.

Figure B-2. *Git commit in git-cola*

You can view a log of your commits with the `git log` command.

```
$ git log
```

Press Q to exit your Git log screen.
In git-cola, select View ➤ DAG to view your log.

Reverting Changes

Git's stated goal is to provide version tracking. That means it lets you keep a record of all the changes made to files, allowing you to revert, or undo, a change when, for instance, some code you thought worked well later reveals a serious bug.

There are many ways to access the history of a Git repository, and in practice, you might have to search the Internet for the best way to grab data from an older version. The most important thing is understanding the basic principles of the process.

To demonstrate, you need a file that's changed. Open your hello.lua file and change its text from hello world to hello git. If you prefer to do that in the terminal, you can.

```
$ sed -i 's/world/git/' hello.lua
```

However you choose to make the change, verify that the file has been altered.

```
bash-4.3$ git diff hello.lua
diff --git a/hello.lua b/hello.lua
index 3b18e51..8d0e412 100644
--- a/hello.lua
+++ b/hello.lua
@@ -1 +1 @@
-print('hello world')
+print('hello git')
```

In git-cola, the Status and Diff panels (see Figure B-3) show what has changed.

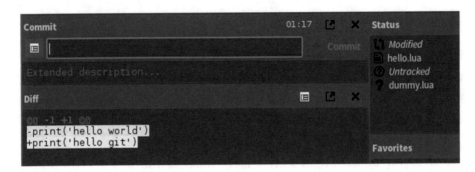

Figure B-3. *Git diff in git-cola*

Look at the state of your repository.

```
$ git status
On branch master
Changes not staged for commit:
  (use "git add <file>..." to update what will be committed)
  (use "git checkout -- <file>..." to discard changes in
  working directory)
        modified:   hello.lua

Untracked files:
  (use "git add <file>..." to include in what will be committed)
        dummy.lua

no changes added to commit (use "git add" and/or "git commit -a")
```

You can see from Git's report that the hello.lua file has been modified but not yet committed, and that the dummy.lua file exists, but it is not being tracked by Git at all.

Restoring with git reset

At this point, with a file that has changed but has not yet been committed, you can reset your repository state back to the last known committed version with the git reset command.

```
$ git reset --hard HEAD
```

The --hard HEAD options tell Git to wipe the slate clean and to reset all tracked files to their state as of the latest commit. This is important to understand, because a git reset doesn't just reset one file, but *all* the files in your repository. This is very efficient if you have spoiled multiple files in your repository, and you want to start from a safe place again, yet it's overkill and possibly detrimental if you have many good changes but you only want to reset one or two files.

Confirm that hello.lua is back to its original state.

```
$ lua ./hello.lua
hello world
```

The dummy.lua file remains entirely unaffected by your reset because it is not being tracked by Git.

```
$ git status
...
Untracked files:
        dummy.lua
```

Restoring with git checkout

If you only want to resurrect one or two files from your history, then use the git checkout command. The checkout option manipulates a file tree, which includes pulling a file from a previous commit into your current workspace.

To demonstrate this, change the file again and then commit the change.

```
$ sed -i 's/world/git/' hello.lua
$ git diff
...
-hello world
+hello git
$ git add hello.lua
$ git commit --message "changed world to git"
```

Now assume that you need to restore hello.lua to its original state. You can't reset, because reset always restores the latest commit.

First, use git log to obtain the unique ID (or *hash*, in technical terminology) of each commit. The hashes in this example and your workspace may differ.

```
$ git log --oneline
42e6b85 (HEAD -> master) changed world to git
ef5288a created hello.lua
```

The commit you want to restore from is not the latest (the one marked HEAD, at the top of the log), but the original commit, with the ef5288a hash.

The git checkout command can take a hash and a specific file name as an argument. To signal Git that you are giving it a file name, however, you must use two dashes as a break point in the command.

```
$ git checkout ef5288a -- hello.lua
```

Confirm that your file has changed back to its original form.

```
$ cat hello.lua
hello world
```

If you're happy with your new old file, then you can add it and then commit it back into your master timeline.

The dummy.lua file is still untouched, because it isn't being tracked by Git.

To perform the same operation in git-cola, select View ➤ DAG to launch the Git log interface so that you can find the file that you want to restore. Once you've located it, right-click it and select Grab File (see Figure B-4), and then save the file to your drive.

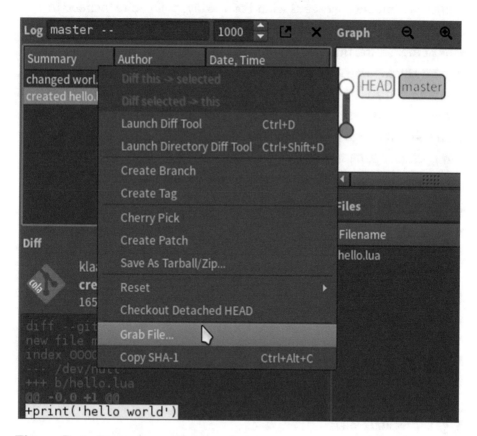

Figure B-4. *Restoring with git-cola*

git branch

When you reach a point that involves many changes to many different files, erasing mistakes with resets and checkouts becomes complex. If there are several people working on a single code base, then resets and checkouts become nearly impossible due to all the changes constantly happening. Luckily, Git provides an infinite number of workspaces, called a *branch*.

When Git initializes a repository, it creates a branch named `master`. A branch is meant to serve as a kind of overlay, or if you're inclined to science fiction, an alternate timeline or parallel universe. Branches let you look at the natural timeline of your Git repository and then "branch" off into any direction you think you might want to go. If the work you're doing in a branch turns out to be less successful than expected, you can abandon the branch and return to the original master timeline, but if it goes well, then you can merge it into the master—*even if the master timeline has changed since you last left it.*

To test this out, first confirm that a master branch exists.

```
$ git branch
* master
```

Create a new branch.

```
$ git branch dev
$ git branch
dev
* master
```

And then switch to the new branch.

```
$ git checkout dev
$ ls
dummy.lua hello.lua
```

To do this in git-cola, select Branch ➤ Create and create a new branch called dev with all the default options. You are automatically switched to your new branch, as indicated by the star icon in the Branches panel.

Make a change to hello.lua.

```
$ echo "print('I am practising Git')" >> hello.lua
```

Confirm that your change has been made.

```
$ git diff hello.lua
diff --git a/hello.lua b/hello.lua
index 3b18e51..0eb0a16 100644
--- a/hello.lua
+++ b/hello.lua
@@ -1 +1,2 @@
 print('hello world')
+print('I am practising Git')
```

Add and commit your change, and finally, add dummy.lua to your repository.

```
$ git add hello.lua dummy.lua
$ git commit -m "added a second line to hello.lua"
```

Get a summary of your dev branch.

```
$ git log --oneline
db5968c (HEAD -> dev) added a second line to hello.lua
42e6b85 (master) changed world to git
ef5288a created hello.lua
$ lua ./hello.lua
hello world
I am practising Git
$ lua ./dummy.lua
Dummy file
```

Now check out the master branch to see what your original timeline is like.

```
$ git checkout master
```

In git-cola, right-click the master branch in the Branches panel and select Checkout.

View your Git log in the terminal, or use DAG in git-cola.

```
$ git log --oneline
42e6b85 (HEAD -> master) changed world to git
ef5288a created hello.lua
$ lua ./hello.lua
hello world
$ lua ./dummy.lua
lua: cannot open ./dummy.lua: No such file or directory
```

The change that you made to hello.lua in the dev branch doesn't exist in your master branch, and the dummy.lua has seemingly vanished entirely.

You haven't lost your work—it just doesn't exist in this workspace. The version of hello.lua in the master branch is the original version, before you added a second line. And dummy.lua is no longer floating around the repository; it has been added to the dev branch exclusively so that it no longer shows up as an untracked file in the master branch.

Jump back over to your dev branch again to verify this.

```
$ git checkout dev
$ git log --oneline
db5968c (HEAD -> dev) added a second line to hello.lua
42e6b85 (master) changed world to git
ef5288a created hello.lua
$ lua ./hello.lua
```

```
hello world
I am practising Git
$ lua ./dummy.lua
Dummy file
```

Generally, you can and should work with Git branches so that you always have a safe, functional code base at the core of your project.

git merge

When two Git branches have diverged, at some point you might want to merge them together. This is a common task in software development just before a release date; the development branch is merged into an official release branch, and then the update is announced to users.

When you're ready to merge two branches, check out the *target* branch—the one you want to bring your work into.

```
$ git checkout master
$ git merge dev
```

In git-cola, the process is similar: check out the master branch, and then right-click the dev branch and select "Merge into current branch" (see Figure B-5).

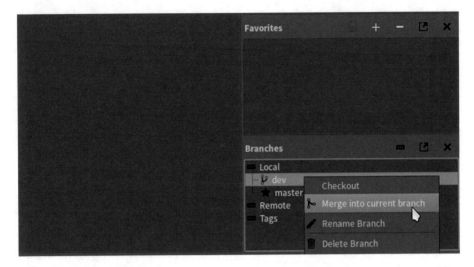

Figure B-5. *Git merge with git-cola*

Verify that the merge has brought in all of your changes.

```
$ ls
dummy.lua hello.lua
$ lua ./hello.lua
hello world
I am practising Git
$ lua ./dummy.lua
Dummy file
```

This is a common workflow in software development: clone a Git repository, create a personal branch for yourself, do your work, and then merge your work into the master branch. When you're finished with a branch, you can delete it.

```
$ git branch --delete dev
Deleted branch dev (was b5dbe64).
```

git push

Using Git locally on your Pi is not very different from using it with a coding website like GitLab or GitHub. The most significant difference with Git hosting sites is that you must also perform a `git push` in order to upload the state of your repository to your Git hosting site. For example, if you had a Git repository on GitLab for this practice exercise, the final step would be

```
$ git push origin HEAD
```

In this example, `origin` is the default alias for your Git hosting site, whether it's GitLab, NotABug.org, GitHub, or any other service. In this example, the term `HEAD` refers to *the current commit.*

As with Lua, practice with Git makes perfect. It's a big system with lots of options and many different ways to achieve many different results. As long as you commit your work often, you run little chance of losing work by mistake, and you stand a good chance of recovering work that's been spoiled by buggy code. Understanding how Git works is what enables you to ask sensible and clear questions when looking online for specific commands.

Index

© Seth Kenlon 2019
S. Kenlon, *Developing Games on the Raspberry Pi*,
https://doi.org/10.1007/978-1-4842-4170-7

H

I

Printed in the United States
By Bookmasters